Harriet Scott, Alexander Walker Scott

Australian Lepidoptera and Their Transformations

Drawn from the life. Vol 2.

Harriet Scott, Alexander Walker Scott

Australian Lepidoptera and Their Transformations
Drawn from the life. Vol 2.

ISBN/EAN: 9783337315504

Printed in Europe, USA, Canada, Australia, Japan

Cover: Foto ©Thomas Meinert / pixelio.de

More available books at **www.hansebooks.com**

AUSTRALIAN MUSEUM, SYDNEY.

AUSTRALIAN LEPIDOPTERA

AND THEIR TRANSFORMATIONS,

BY THE LATE

ALEXANDER WALKER SCOTT:

With Illustrations drawn from the life by his Daughters,

HARRIET MORGAN AND HELENA FORDE.

VOL. II.

EDITED AND REVISED

BY

HELENA FORDE AND ARTHUR SIDNEY OLLIFF.

SYDNEY:
PRINTED BY ORDER OF THE TRUSTEES.
E. P. RAMSAY, SUCCEEDED BY R. ETHERIDGE, JUNR.,
CURATOR.
1890 - 1898.

INTRODUCTION.

The Manuscripts and Drawings of the late Mr. A. W. Scott relating to the life-histories of the Australian Lepidoptera, having passed into the possession of the Trustees of the Australian Museum, it was decided to continue the publication, and the work of editing and revising the Notes was entrusted to the late Mr. A. Sidney Olliff, then Entomologist to the Museum, and afterwards to the Department of Agriculture, and Mrs. H. Forde, a daughter of the late Mr. Scott. Four Parts have been issued, of which the dates of Publication are:—

Part 1. 30 April, 1890.
2. 28 February, 1891.
3. 30 November, 1891.
4. 31 May, 1893.

The death of Mr. Olliff, the imperfect state of the remainder of the Notes, and the retirement of Mrs. Forde, brought the work to a standstill, and the Trustees determined to discontinue it for the present. The four Parts above referred to, with the Title Page and Index issued herewith, will therefore form Vol. II. of Mr. A. W. Scott's "Australian Lepidoptera." Volume I. was published in London in 1864.

R. ETHERIDGE, Junr.,
Curator.

Sydney, 31st October, 1898.

BIOGRAPHICAL NOTICE.

ALEXANDER WALKER SCOTT was born at Bombay on the 10th November, 1800, and was the second son of Helenus Scott, M.D., head of the Bombay Medical Staff, and a well-known contributor to medical and scientific literature. He was educated in England, graduating at Peterhouse, Cambridge, as B.A. in 1821, and M.A. in 1824. Shortly afterwards he left England for New South Wales, taking up his residence first in Sydney, but eventually settling upon Ash Island, on the Lower Hunter River, near Newcastle. He represented various local constituencies in the Legislative Assembly, from 1856 to 1861, when he was appointed a member of the first Legislative Council under the new constitution. He was a Trustee of the Australian Museum from 1862 to 1879, when he resigned in consequence of ill health; as one of the original members and sometime President of the Entomological Society of New South Wales, he contributed various papers on entomological subjects to its Transactions, and also to the Proceedings of the Zoological Society of London. In 1864 he published the first three parts of his *Australian Lepidoptera*; and in 1873 a treatise on *Mammalia, Recent and Extinct* (Class Pinnata). He was engaged at the time of his death, which took place at Sydney on November 1st, 1883, upon a Catalogue of the Seals and Whales in the collection of the Australian Museum.

VOLUME II, PART I.
(APRIL 30, 1890.)

AUSTRALIAN MUSEUM, SYDNEY.

PRICE, 15/-

Australian Lepidoptera
with their
Transformations

BY THE LATE
A. W. SCOTT,
EDITED AND REVISED
BY
A. SIDNEY OLLIFF AND HELENA FORDE.

SYDNEY:
PRINTED BY ORDER OF THE TRUSTEES.
1890.

PREFACE.

The Trustees of the Australian Museum, in the year 1888, having determined that in the interests of entomological science, the important mass of information regarding the transformations of one of the most noticeable and beautiful orders of insects —the result of years of patient observation and labour—should be made known with as little delay as possible, decided that the valuable manuscripts and drawings relating to the life-histories of our native butterflies and moths, which they acquired by purchase in 1884 from the Executors of the late Alexander Walker Scott, should be made available to students of Entomology and the public. In pursuance of this decision they determined that the manuscripts and the drawings should be published; and at a meeting held on the 4th December, 1888, they decided that the publication should take the form of a continuation of the work of which three parts were issued by Mr. Scott, in 1864, under the title *Australian Lepidoptera and their Transformations*. The task of editing and revising the manuscripts was entrusted to us as co-editors, and the entomological notes and descriptions left by Mr. Scott, comprised in six note-books, and a large collection of drawings, were placed in our hands.

The manuscripts contain a series of observations, commencing in 1838 and ending in 1864, made principally in the neighbourhood of Sydney and in the Lower Hunter district, on many hundreds of Lepidoptera; and when it is borne in mind that nothing had been done towards elucidating the life-histories of the Australian Lepidoptera since 1805, when John William Lewin published his *Natural History of Lepidopterous Insects of New South Wales*, it is obvious that many of the insects described and named by Mr. Scott were new to science. The large additions made, during the last quarter of a century, to entomological literature, and the great amount of work accomplished during the same period by systematic naturalists, have necessarily brought about great changes in the nomenclature and classification of species; and we have therefore found it necessary, in revising the manuscripts, to substitute the nomenclature employed by recent writers, and to omit all those passages which relate to questions of classification or the limits of genera as then constituted. Indeed it may be said once for all, that the editors are entirely responsible for the nomenclature adopted in this continuation of Mr. Scott's work, and also for the bibliographical references at the head of each description. Wherever it seemed to us desirable, in order to avoid confusion, we have endeavoured to bring the terminology into conformity with modern usage; and wherever we are able to add anything to the life-histories of the species described in the work, from our own knowledge or from other sources, we have done so, distinguishing our remarks from those of the author by enclosing them within brackets [ ], or appending our respective initials. With these exceptions we have closely followed the text of the original manuscripts, making only such verbal alterations as appeared to us necessary.

Plates X. to XXI., used in the present work, were lithographed and printed in Sydney, previous to 1864, with a view to the continuous issue of the work, which will account for discrepancies between names used on the plates and those adopted in the text. As the Trustees of the Australian Museum felt bound to utilize these plates, which had been executed at considerable expense and had the advantage of being the work of the original artists, this discrepancy could not be avoided; but no inconvenience will arise on this account, as in every instance an explanation is given, not only in the text, but also on the explanation facing each plate.

Finally it is hoped that readers will bear in mind the difficulties which always attend a posthumous publication, enhanced in this case, by the long interval of time which elapsed before the manuscripts became the property of the Australian Museum, an interval moreover (1864-1884) singularly barren in workers in this particular field. Those early workers who, like John Abbot in Georgia, Johann Christian Sepp in Surinam, General Hardwicke in India, and Thomas Horsfield in Java, turned their attention to the laborious pursuit of insect biology, deserve some gratitude from those who come after them, and we feel sure that in this connection the name of Alexander Walker Scott will be honourably remembered.

A. SIDNEY OLLIFF.
HELENA FORDE.

Sydney: January 1st, 1890.

AUSTRALIAN LEPIDOPTERA.

VOL. II.

INDEX.

NOTE.—Species are distinguished by having the *Generic* name in capital and small capital letters, and the *Specific* name in italics, thus: CŒQUOSA *triangularis*: Synonyms are printed in full italics: *Sphinx triangularis;* names of food plants and general terms, in Roman: Vitis antarctica, Papilio, etc.

	PAGE
abeimilis, HOLOCHILA	9, 10
" *Polygyna*	9
Acacia decurrens	33
Acheronia triangularis	5
Acronychia laueri	33, 34
" *lævis*	12
Ænotheras	14, 16
Agarista	18
AGARISTA *agricola*	18
" *casuarinæ*	18
" *Donovani*	16
Agarista frontinus	23
AGARISTA *glycinæ*	15, 17
" *latina*	17
" *Lewini*	14, 15, 16
Agarista astorius	28
agricola, AGARISTA	18
albo-fasciata, *Catocala*	26
alculus, LAMPIDES	9, 10
" *Lycæna*	10
amœna, *Eulophoncampe*	28
anacardioides, Cupania	9, 10, 33
anactus, PAPILIO	19
augasii, *Euplœa*	20
Ancœla sabbulatica	35
Anona	33
" *cherenolia*	22
antarctica, Vitis	17
Antheræa	11, 12, 31
ANTHERÆA *astrophela*	11, 12
" *eucalypti*	12
" *helena*	12
" *janetta*	11, 12
Antheræa simplex	11
Apple, Custard	22
Asclepiadeæ	20
Ash tree (native)	26
" native	11
astrophela, ANTHERÆA	11, 12
atkinsoni, *Ophideres*	6
atrata, Spenocola	23
attenia, *Boarmia*	35
aurantium, Citron	19, 31
australasia, METANIMAN	5
australis, Indigofera	10
" Livistona	13, 14
Balsam (common)	14
Balsams	16
Bankaim	8
"Banggala Palm"	13
baueri, Acronychia	33, 34
Boarmia attenia	35
" *psychastis*	33
bariam, LYCÆNA	9, 10, 11
bariam, Papilio	10

	PAGE
Brachypylous triangularis	5
Breynia oblongifolia	23, 24
brownii, Scolopia	12
Cabbage tree	13
cabbalistica, Anocœla	25
camels pule, Geometra	33
camphor laurel (the)	32
Camphor tree	21
Canophora officinalis	21
Catocala albo-fasciata	26
" *fusca*	24
Cœsythia paniculata	9
ceanyths, Polygynous	9
casuarinus, AGARISTA	18
Chanapa corinna	20
CHARAXIA *retinia*	8
" *lignicora*	8
" *ramosyi*	8
" *scripta*	8
" *splendens*	8
CHARAXES *sempronius*	21
Cheiropteryx expolitus	27
cheremolia, Anona	22
chordon, Papilio	21
CHRYSOPHANUS *erinna*	9
Cissus	7, 15, 16
Citron leaves	19
Citrus aurantium	19, 31
Cnoptera Polygynous	8, 9
Colutea frutescens	11
communis, Phragmites	14
consequana, Wisteria	9
Convolvulus	35
corocha, Hesperia	12
corinna, Chanapa	20
" *Danaus*	20
Cudrania javanensis	11
Cupania anacardioides	9, 10, 33
Custard Apple	22
damoites, Papilio	10
Danaida	20
Danais *corinna*	20
DARALA *hamata*	28
decurrens, Acacia	33
destinataria, Gnophos	35
" SELIDOSEMA	35
disperdita, Tephrosia	34
Dodonœa viscosa	8
donovani, AGARISTA	16
Dolichos	11
elata, Podocarpus	11, 12
elegans, Ptychosperma	13
Elæocarpus obovatus	11, 26
Epilobium *junceum*	14, 16

	PAGE
Epilobium tetragonum	15
erectheus, PAPILIO	19
erinna, CHRYSOPHANUS	9
" *Papilio*	9
erithminus, Papilio	30, 31
Eucalypti	27
eucalypti, ANTHERÆA	12
Eucalyptus	27, 28
Eugenia	13
Eulophocampe amœna	28
Euplœa augasii	20
EUPLŒA *corinna*	20
eurypylus, Papilio	22
eremita, CHARAXIA	8
" *Phlœisopsyche*	6
expolitus, Cheloptery	27
PODIRA *astorius*	25
frequens, Polyommatus	10
frontinus, Agarista	23
" OPHIURA ?	23, 24
" *Papilio*	23
frutescens, Colutea	11
fusca, Catocala	24
fulionica, OPHIDERES	6, 7
"Fustic"	11
galegifolia, Swainsona	11
Geijera salicifolia	21, 32, 31, 32
Geometra cameli-pile	33
" *gilca*	33
" *lentiginosa*	35
" *recta-fasciata*	34
"*gibbung*"	6
gilca, Geometra	33
SELIDOSEMA	33
glabrum, Menispermum	7
glycinæ, AGARISTA	15, 17
" *Phalænoides*	15
Gnaphalium luteoalbum	16
Gnophos destinataria	35
Goniloba vulpecula	12
graveolens, Ruta	19
greyana, *Swainsona*	11
Haloragis tetartoides	17, 16
hamata, DARALA	28
Hardenbergia monophylla	16
harveyanum, Karampetalum	6
helena, ANTHERÆA	12
holinepis, OCHSIIA	27, 28
Hemeraphila luxuria	34
hernandiafolia, Stephania	6, 35, 36
Hesperia coroeba	12
" *phineus*	13
hispida, Robinia	9
HOLOCHILA *abeimilis*	9, 10
Ichnæmon	34

INDEX—Continued.

	PAGE
Indigofera australis	10
indirecta, Tephrosia	35
janetta, ANTHERAA	11, 12
javanensis, Oudrania	11
junceum, Epilobium	14, 15
Junonia	30
lævis, Acronychia	12
LAMPIDES alexius	9, 10
lanceolata, Persoonia	6
latina, AGARISTA	17
latinus, Phalœna	17
laurel, camphor	32
leguminis, Lycœna	10
leiocaryum, Nephelium	12, 13
leutigenum, Grumetra	35
Leptospermum scoparium	34, 35
lewini, AGARISTA	14, 15, 16
ligniveva, CHARAGIA	8
Livistona australis	13, 14
longifolia, Notelæa	12
luteoalbum, Gnaphalium	16
lusoria, Hemerophila	34
,, SELIDOSEMA	34
Lycœna alculus	10
LYCŒNA bœtica	9, 10, 11
Lycœna leguminis	10
lycaon, PAPILIO	22
maclayanus, PAPILIO	21, 31, 32
Macrodenia suaveolens	20, 25
Menispermum glabrum	7
METAMINAS australasia	5
Mœnas salaminia	6
monophylla, Hardenbergia	16
myops, OPHUSA	24
native ash	11
,, pine	11
Nephelium leiocaryum	12, 13
Nerium (the)	25
NETROCORYNE repanda	12
Noctua salaminia	6
,, scapularis	25
Notolæa longifolia	12
oblongifolia, Brynia	23, 24
obovata, Elæocarpus	11, 26
OCHESIA heliaspis	27, 28
officinalis, Camphora	21
Oleander tree	25
Ophideres	7
Ophideres atkinsoni	6
OPHIDERES fullonica	6, 7

	PAGE
OPHIDERES salaminia	6, 7
OPHIUSA (f) frontinus	23, 24
,, myops	24
,, smee	26
Orange (the)	19, 31, 32
orange-fly	7
osiorius, Agaristia	25
,, FODINA	25
,, Phalœna	25
Palm, "Bangla"	13
palmarum, Pamphila	13
Palms (the)	14
Pamphila palmarum	13
Panicalata, Casuyba	9
PAPILIO anactus	19
Papilio bœricus	10
,, choreton	21
,, damarius	10
PAPILIO ærathous	19
Papilio erinus	9
,, erichmius	30, 31
,, eurypylus	22
,, frontinus	23
PAPILIO lycaon	22
,, maclayanus	21, 31, 32
Papilio phineus	12
PAPILIO serpedon	21, 23, 32
Papilio scoltianus	31
PAPILIO sthenelus	30
Pea, Poison	11
Persoonia lanceolata	6
Persoonia	6
Phalœna latinus	17
,, Noctua salaminia	6
,, ostorius	25
Phalœnoides glycine	15
,, phineus, Papilio	13
,, Hesperia	13
Phloiopsyche sximia	8
Phragmites communis	14
pine, native	11
Podocarpus elata	11, 12
Polycyma abrimilis	9
,, oxanthe	9
Polygonatus frequens	10
Poison Pea	11
psychastis, Bœarmia	33
Ptychosperma alcyana	13
ramosyl, CHARAGIA	8
recto-fasciata, Oscenatra	34

	PAGE
repanda, NETROCORYNE	12
Robinia hispida	9
Ruta graveolens	19
salaminia, Mœnas	6
,, Noctua	6
,, Ophideres	6, 7
,, Phalœna Noctua	6
salicifolia, Grijera	21, 22, 31, 32
Salvia	31
Sarcopetalum harveyanum	6
serpedon, PAPILIO	21, 23, 32
scopularis, Noctua	25
Scolopia brownii	12
scoparium, Leptospermum	34, 35
scotianus, Papilio	31
scripta, CHARAGIA	8
SELIDOSEMA destinataria	35
,, gilva	33
,, lusaria	34
,, thermea	33
scoporinus, CHARAXES	21
smee, OPHIUSA	26
simplex, Antheræa	11
Spanocala atrata	23
Sphinx triangularis	5
splendens, CHARAGIA	8
Stephania hernandifolia	6, 35, 36
sthenelus, PAPILIO	30
suaveolens, Macrdenia	20, 25
Swainsona	11
Swainsona greyana	11
,, galegifolia	11
Tephrosia dispersita	34
,, indirecta	35
,, vagaria	35
tetragonum, Epilobium	15
teucrinidra, Halonagia	17, 18
triangularis, Achrontia	5
,, Brachygloss	5
,, Cœquoss	5, 6
,, Sphinx	5
Trypeta	7
thermea, SELIDOSEMA	33
vagaria, Tephrosia	35
viscosa, Dodonea	6
Vitis	18
,, antarctica	17
vulpecula, Genilobe	6
Wistaria consequana	9

LIST OF PLATES.

PLATE 10.
CŒQUOSA TRIANGULARIS.

PLATE 11.
OPHIDERES ATKINSONI = O. salaminia, in text.
PHLOIOPSYCHE EXIMIA = Charagia eximia, in text.

PLATE 12.
POLYCYMA CAMYTHE = Chrysophanus erinus, in ext.
,, ABRIMILIS = Holochila abrimilis, in text.
POLYOMMATUS FREQUENS = Lampides alculus, in ext.
LYCÆNA LEGUMINIS = L. bœtica, in text.

PLATE 13.
ANTHERÆA SIMPLEX = A. astrophela, in text.

PLATE 14.
HESPERIA CORNERA = Netrocoryne repanda, in text.
PAMPHILA PALMARUM = P. phineus, in text.

PLATE 15.
AGARISTA LEWINI.
,, GLYCINE.
,, DONOVANI.
,, LATINA.

PLATE 16.
PAPILIO ANACTUS.
DANAIS CORINNA = Euploea corinna, in text.

PLATE 17.
PAPILIO SARPEDON.
,, EURYPYLUS = P. lycaon, in text.

PLATE 18.
SPANOCALA ATRATA = Ophiusa (f) frontinus, in text.
CATOCALA FUSCI = Ophiusa myops, in text.
ANOCALA CASSALISTICA = Fodina ostorius, in text.
CATOCALA ALBO-FASCIATA = Ophiusa smee, in text.

PLATE 19.
CHELEPTERYX REPOLITUS = Ocneria heliaspis, in text.
EULOPHOCAMPE ANOMA = Darala humata, in text.

PLATE 20.
PAPILIO STHENELUS.
,, MACLEAYANUS.

PLATE 21.
GEOMETRA CAMELI-PILO = Selidosema thermea, in text.
,, GILVA = ,, gilva, in text.
,, LENTIGINOSA = ,, destinataria, in text.
,, RECTO-FASCIATA = ,, lusaria, in text.

AUSTRALIAN LEPIDOPTERA

AND THEIR

TRANSFORMATIONS.

OEQUOSA TRIANGULARIS, Donovan.—(Plate X.)

Sphinx triangularis, Donovan, Ins. New Holl., pl. 33, fig. 2 (1805).
Acherontia triangularis, Boisduval, Voy. de d'Astrolabe, Ent., p. 181 (1832).
Brachyglossa triangularis, Boisduval, Hist. Nat. Ins., Spéc. Gén., Lep., Vol. I., pl. 16, fig. 2 (1836); Spéc. Gen. Lép. Hét. (Spding.), I., p. 9 (1874).
Coequosa triangularis, Walker, Cat. Lep. Het. Brit. Mus., viii., p. 237 (1856).
LIFE-HISTORY: Boisduval, Spéc. Gén. Lép. Hét.. I., p. 10 (1874); a brief allusion to a drawing by M. Jules Vurreaux.

The caterpillars of this species may be met with from October to December, not only along the line of coast extending on either side of Port Jackson, but also in the Newcastle district, wherever in fact the various species of Banksia and Persoonia abound, yet in point of number they are by no means abundant, being, with the allied *Metamimas australasiæ*, Don., typical insects in all collections of lepidoptera sent from Australia. They have been for many years the especial prey of the collector, the size and showy appearance of the caterpillars, and their habit of taking up an exposed position on the branch on which they happen to be feeding, almost compelling observation. Their destruction may also be aided by a vulgar belief in the noxious qualities of the caterpillar, partly caused by its habit, when molested, of lashing its body violently from side to side, as if eager to attack its opponent, while the spiny, rough skin, and the large shining black spots near the tail—commonly mistaken for eyes—add greatly to its vicious appearance.

The full grown or mature larva measures, (*) according to sex, from 4¾ to 5 inches. The body is cylindrical and tapers towards the head; the posterior portion being thick, rounded above, and entirely destitute of caudal horn or protuberance. Although they correspond exactly in general marking, they vary much in colour, and we therefore in our present plate figure two of the extremes, in order that those of intermediate shades may be easily recognised. One is of a rich bright green, the whole surface closely covered with small white granulations, disposed transversely, affording to the eye and touch a strong resemblance to shagreen. On each side are seven oblique, yellowish-white bands relieved anteriorly by dark blue, with a yellowish-white, indistinct, oblique band on the thoracic segments, extending from below the middle of the third segment to behind the head, and a similar band on the penultimate segment. Immediately above the caudal feet there is a distinct bright raised black spot, bearing an exact resemblance to the pupil of an eye, so much so indeed, that the casual observer is invariably misled, and points to the posterior portion of the body as the head of the animal. Along the back are two longitudinal rows of yellowish-white spines, fourteen on each segment (seven on each side), and over the oblique bands of yellow, a row of similar spines, passing in a continuous line through two segments, from the ventral to the dorsal aspect of the caterpillar, and another row runs from head to tail just above the feet on each side. The head is green, conical, and slightly bifurcate in front, the terminal portion being of a rusty yellow.

The other larva is of a pale straw-colour throughout, with seven short oblique bands on each side of white, edged broadly with bright purple, the first and last of which are indistinct. A clear bluish-green tint occupies the back. In other respects the insect agrees with the form already described.

The chrysalis (fig. 1) is contained within a nest, on the surface of the ground, formed of dead leaves joined together by a strong but coarse web. It measures 2¼ inches in length, is of a deep shining black with reddish brown segmental divisions, and in form approximates more to the pupæ of the larger Bombycidæ than to those of the Sphingidæ. The perfect insects take wing principally in January and February, although, like most other species, they may be found occasionally during the whole of the summer months. In expanse they attain to six inches.

The *Antennæ* ....long, somewhat setaceous, slightly thickest in the middle, and terminated by a few setæ; of the male (fig. 2) covered posteriorly with scales, anteriorly with transverse rows of ciliations arranged in pairs, the upper row being longest and entire—the lower row disunited in the middle, recurving to each other at their tips; of the female covered with scales above and naked beneath.

---

* [In this and the following descriptions the head is considered separately, and the segments are counted antero-posteriorly from one to twelve. The measurements are in terms of an inch. It is almost unnecessary to add that—a line = .08333 of an inch; a millimetre = .03937 of an inch.—ED.]

The *Maxillæ* ....short.

The *Labial palpi* (fig. 3, male) project forwards and upwards to about three-fourths of the eye; second joint robust, nearly four times the length of the basal; terminal minute, nearly obsolete; the whole covered with hairs which become more bushy at the tip.

The *Legs* ....strong, sparingly clothed with hair (anterior pair, fig. 4, male), second pair with two, and posterior pair (fig. 5, female) with four spurs, the upper pair of the latter exceedingly small and buried in the hair of the tibiæ.

Wings deltoid when at rest, the moth being usually suspended by the anterior feet, a position, we observe, generally adopted by all the Sphingidæ The ground colour of the fore wings is of a rich reddish brown, having on the centre of each, at the costa, a large triangular patch of deeper brown, strikingly relieved outwardly by a powdered mass of white. The abdominal margin is edged by white, and a white patch at the anal angle. The hind wings are likewise of a deep reddish brown, merging into bright orange yellow towards their base, with a whitish triangular patch at the anal angle, and a whitish marginal fringe. The head, thorax and abdomen are robust, and of an olive-brown colour; the patagia edged with a purplish band, which also proceeds along the scutellum and abdomen. The under surface is ochreous, the triangular patch on the upper side of the fore wings being partially defined, with the space between it and the base orange yellow. A faintly indicated bar of white passes transversely through the disc of each wing.

The plant upon which the caterpillars are represented is the *Persoonia lanceolata* or "gibbung" of the aborigines, to the ripe berries of which they are extremely partial, although to Europeans the fruit is insipid and worthless.

The original of the slight sketch, introduced into this plate, is from the able pencil of the late Mr. Conrad Martens, whose finished drawings of Australian scenery are so well known. The view represents the entrance of Port Jackson, with the old Sydney Lighthouse, which formerly occupied the site of the Macquarie Light at South Head.

[*C. triangularis* is rather widely distributed in Australia, but as far as we are aware it does not extend its range into New Guinea or the adjacent islands; nor has it, as far as we know, been observed in Tasmania. It is particularly abundant on the seaboard side of the great chain of mountains which borders the entire eastern coast-line of Australia, occurring from Cape York, at one extremity of the continent, to Wilson's Promontory at the other. It may be of interest to add that Mr. Scott has the following note with regard to a batch of *C. triangularis* larvæ which he found in December, 1840:—"These caterpillars," he says, "had the usual changes of skin, but at the last one seemed generally to suffer much. Several remained six days previous to casting the skin, and six days after, without eating."]

OPHIDERES SALAMINIA, Cramer.—(Plate XI.)

Phalæna Noctua salaminia, Cramer, Pap. Exot., II., p. 117, pl. clxxiv., fig. A (1779); Clerk, Icones, pl. xlviii., fig. 5, 6.
Noctua salaminia, Fabricius, Syst. Ent., III., p. 17 (1794).
Mænas salaminia, Hubner, Verz. bek. Schmett., p. 261; Moore, Trans. Zool. Soc., London, XI., p. 71, pl. xiv., fig. 2 (1881); Lep. Ceylon, III., p. 134, pl. 161, fig. 1 (1884).
Ophideres salaminia, Guenée, Spec. Gen. Lep., Noct., VII., p. 115; Walker, Cat. Lep. Het. B.M., XIII., p. 1228 (1857).
Ophideres atkinsoni, Scott, MS.
LIFE-HISTORY: Moore, Trans. Zool. Soc., London, XI., pl. xii., fig. 3, 3a, 3b, larva and pupa (figures only) from Allipore (Grote), and Java (Horsfield); Lep. Ceylon, III., p. 134, pl. 161, fig. 1b (1884).

In February we found on Ash Island, Lower Hunter River, feeding on the *Sarcopetalum harveyanum*, a brood of about twenty half-grown larvæ, which, from their similarity of markings and general contour, we at once referred to *Ophideres fullonica*. In course of time, however, one of the number exhibited such marked divergence in colouring from its companions, that we were led to suspect the presence of a second species, a surmise which ultimately proved correct. Three months later we fortunately secured another full grown larva of a reddish colour, and since then several fine specimens have been forwarded to us from Singleton, in the Upper Hunter district, where they were captured feeding on *Stephania hernandiæfolia*, another Menispermaceous plant.

The full grown larva is very handsome, although both in colour and markings it is inferior to *Ophideres fullonica*. It is throughout of a deep rich velvety-black, minutely powdered with small spots of white, pale blue, and straw colour, the whole forming a rich combination to which the pencil cannot do justice. On each side of the fifth and sixth segments is a gaudy ocellus, possessing a black pupil with a blue centre, and an iris yellowish above and saturnine-red below. On the back between the ocelli are two oval white spots, one on each segment, and there is a similar white spot on the fourth segment. The penultimate segment bears a reddish prominence, from which proceeds along each side a delicate tracery of white, resembling the fine fibrous roots of a plant; and a similar but larger tracery rises obliquely upwards from the last of the abdominal feet and passes over the adjoining segment. Dull reddish indistinct spots are placed one on each segment, in the region of the stigmata, and are connected by a flexuous row of small pale straw coloured spots. The head of the caterpillar is black, and the terminal portions of the feet, both thoracic and abdominal, are dull brownish-red. Another caterpillar was of a dull reddish hue, and the white dorsal spots between the ocelli and on the fourth segment were almost obsolete; and a like diversity in colouring existed in those sent to us from Singleton. These larvæ are half-loopers, the first pair of abdominal feet being nearly obsolete: when at rest they assume fantastic attitudes, generally supporting themselves entirely by their abdominal feet, with the head and anterior segments curved towards the chest, and the posterior extremity elevated. When touched they instantly fall to the ground, where they remain as if feigning death, until danger is past. In length they are about 3¼ inches; in form cylindrical, not flat beneath, and very fleshy and soft to the touch. The cocoon is formed of leaves so loosely woven together as to afford but a frail protection to the chrysalis, so much so that, if handled, it is apt to fall through. The chrysalis (fig. 1) is 1½ inch in length, and throughout of a shining black. The perfect insect measures nearly 3¾ inches in expanse of wings, and remains in the pupa state for about two months.

The *Antennæ* ....are long, setaceous, basal half almost naked, thence with a row of fine setæ on each side to the apex, which is terminated by a tuft of setæ.

The *Maxillæ* ....(fig. 2) short and thick, the basal portion naked, the remainder fringed externally with short cilia, and internally with a few setæ, which are succeeded by serrations immediately behind the sharply pointed tip.*

The *Labial palpi* (figs. 3 and 4) with the terminal joint conical, very small, basal and middle joints more robust, the latter about twice the length of the former; the whole closely covered with hair, and projecting upwards and forwards to about even with the top of the head.

The *Legs* ....powerful; tibiæ of anterior (fig. 5) and posterior (fig. 6) pairs pilose, the latter armed with four long spurs; second pairs nearly naked, and with two apical spurs.

These moths are nocturnal, but, like other members of the family, if disturbed during the heat of the day, they can fly not only with rapidity, but with great certainty as to direction. The fore wings of this conspicuous insect are trigonate and entire, with the abdominal margin undulating, concave at the inner angle, and towards the base, interrupted by an angular tuft of scales, from which, including the base, springs a very broad subcostal band ending in a point at the tip of the wing. This band is of brilliant silver, delicately striated transversely with lilac lines, and becoming dark green along the costa. A somewhat similar but narrower band, attenuated at the extremities, extends along the outer margin. The intermediate triangular space is dark satiny green, assuming a lustrous brown or golden hue in different lights. A reddish-brown line between the third median nervule and submedian nervure reaches from band to band. The posterior wings are bright orange, with a broad black apical fimbria which, although interrupted at the anal angle, recurves spirally to the middle of the wing. The outer margin alternately fringed with black and white. The palpi, head, and prothorax are pale lilac; the thorax, eyes, and antennæ greenish, the former much crested; abdomen bright yellow and tufted dorsally. The underside of the forewings is brownish, with the base and a transverse bar across the disc ochreous; the hind wings resemble the upper surface, but are very much paler and duller. Thorax, legs, and abdomen are pale yellowish brown.

This description is taken from living specimens recently born and fresh in their plumage, as the brilliant colours fade rapidly after death.

[*Ophideres salaminia* extends to New Guinea, Java, Singapore, and throughout India, China and Japan. Its larva was reared in Java by Dr. Horsfield on *Cissus*, and Mr. A. Grote has recorded that it feeds on *Menispermum glabrum* at Allipore, near Calcutta; whilst in Ceylon, Mr. F. Moore informs us, it is found on the same food-plant. We have ourselves observed the young larvæ on the former plant at Sydney.]

---

* [Since this description was written, the structure of the proboscis in *Ophideres* has excited considerable interest on account of certain observations which were recorded by M. A. Thozet, of Rockhampton, concerning the capacity for piercing the epicarp of oranges, which he supposed these moths to possess. In a letter in the "Rockhampton Bulletin" (May, 1875), he stated that *O. fullonica* did considerable damage to oranges in Queensland, by puncturing the rind, extracting their juices, and thus causing the fruit to fall. From specimens of the moth forwarded by M. Thozet, detailed accounts of the structure of the proboscis were drawn up by M. J. Kunckel (Ann. Mag. Nat. Hist., 4, xvi., pp. 372-371, 1875) and Mr. Francis Darwin (Q. Journ. Micr. Sc., xv., pp. 364-389, 1875). In both articles reference is made to the manner in which the organ is brought into use. M. Kunckel describes the proboscis as a "veritable auger," while Mr. Darwin says—"It is clear that in using its proboscis the insect must employ a thrusting action, and not any kind of revolving movement; the proboscis must accordingly be considered as a saw, not as an auger or gimlet. It is, in fact, a bayonet shaped saw, and most, therefore, have three cutting edges." Mr. G. L. Pilcher (Cistula Ent. ii., pp.237-240, 1887), who appears to have had opportunities of examining the living insects, states that the *Ophideres* attacks the guava, banana, and peach, as well as the orange. He doubts the capacity of the moth to perforate the skin of the fruit with its proboscis, the instrument appearing to him adapted for enlarging a hole already existing, rather than for boring; and he contends that the *Ophideres* merely enlarges the punctures already made by other insects, especially by the larvæ of the orange fly (*Trypeta*). Excellent figures of the distal extremity of the proboscis of *O. fullonica* and *O. salaminia* will be found in a paper contributed by Mr. R. D. Read to the "Proceedings of the Linnean Society of New South Wales for 1878."—A.S.O.]

CHARAGIA EXIMIA, Scott.—(Plate XI. ♂)

Charagia eximia, Scott, Trans. Entom. Soc., New South Wales, II., p. 35 (1867); description of male.
Phloiopsyche eximia, Scott, MS.
LIFE-HISTORY. Scott, *loc. cit.*

We presented to our readers in Vol. I., Plate 2, two species of Charagia, and we now add another example of this beautiful genus, regretting, however, that we can only figure the male, as we were unfortunately unsuccessful in our attempts to rear most of the caterpillars we had collected, owing to the shrinking of the wood in which they lived.

We purpose to continue the series of these peculiarly Australasian insects, and hope in time to furnish illustrations of the transformations of two of the largest and most conspicuous species, *Charagia Ramsayi* and *C. scripta*. We cannot add anything now in respect to the habits and metamorphoses of this insect, as these agree precisely with the characters we have previously given in detail of this group, and we must consequently refer the reader to our previous remarks for all particulars relating thereto. The larvæ were found at one time in considerable numbers at Ash Island, in the small stems or branches of the *Dodonæa viscosa*, Linn.; but the destruction of these plants in the process of clearing the lands for cultivation in that particular locality, has since rendered the attainment of this species a matter of difficulty to us. This caterpillar is cylindrical and fleshy, except the head and adjoining segment, which are rough and corneous. The segments are muscular and well developed, and of a dull creamy white, tinged with purplish red at their divisions, and also around the various longitudinal wrinkles which are placed at the lower portion of each segment. The caterpillar is also slightly setigerous. The females are about 4½ inches in length, the males smaller.

The chrysalis (fig 1, male) measures rather more than 1½ inch, stoutest at the anterior portion. The colour yellowish-white, becoming dark brown towards the head, where it is rough, corneous, and slightly setigerous: the abdomen encircled with hard ridges. The male of the perfect insect measures 3 inches in expanse.

The *Antennæ* ....(fig. 2, male) very short, setaceous, slightly moniliform, delicately ciliated above, with a few fine setæ beneath.

The *Labial palpi* (figs. 3 and 4) very small, projecting forwards and slightly downwards, and thinly covered with hair; terminal joint minute and conical; basal about one-third less than the second, and somewhat inflated.

The *Legs* ....with the anterior (fig. 5, male) and intermediate pairs long and powerful, densely and compactly clothed with hair; posterior (fig. 6, male) small, weak, covered sparingly with hair; tibiæ furnished exteriorly with a long tuft of golden coloured hair.

The moth, when at rest, suspends itself by its powerful anterior feet, the tips of the wings meeting beneath the abdomen, which is not recurved as in *Charagia lignivora* and *C. splendens* before described.

The superior wings are falcate in a greater degree than in any of our other species, and the ground colour throughout is of a pale emerald green, chastely relieved by a series of numerous short slightly curved lines, exhibiting a chain-like pattern of bright silver disposed transversely, each link, however, being interrupted by the nervures. These lines become, towards the base, more irregular and labyrinthic. A dull golden band, also interrupted by the nervures, passes transversely through the disc, commencing close to the costal, and terminating near the inner margin. The hind wings are of pale bluish green, partially clothed towards the basal portion and abdominal margin with short silvery hairs. The cilia at the outer angle golden brown. The head, prothorax, and patagia, similar in colour to the fore wings; the thorax and abdomen to that of the hind wings, and covered on the upper portion with silvery hairs. Eyes large, projecting, and dark purplish-brown. The underside is of a uniform pale whitish-green, glossed with a golden tinge towards the tips of the wings.

We have represented the male insect and the caterpillar in a branch of the *Dodonæa viscosa*, or Native Hop, so called from the winged seed capsules with which the plant is liberally covered.

During the past ten or twelve years *Charagia eximia* has been obtained by breeding in considerable numbers in the Lower Hunter district. Indeed, for the past two seasons—as I am in a position to state from personal observation—it has been the most abundant species of the genus, not only in that locality, but also in the immediate vicinity of Sydney. Mr. Scott suspected from the large size of some of his larvæ, that the male described above—the only example which he succeeded in rearing—was undersized; but this has not proved to be the case. The males vary from 62 to 60 mm. in expanse, and the females from 100 to 112 mm. The following is a brief description of the latter sex:—

♀ Antennæ brownish red. Head, thorax, apex of abdomen, and the anterior and intermediate legs bright grass-green; basal half of abdomen pinkish salmon colour; posterior legs pinkish yellow. Fore-wing bright grass-green, obscurely mottled with transverse irregular wavy lines between the veins; three moderately large silvery spots beyond the cell, indistinctly encircled with brown, arranged obliquely one behind the other; two very obscure brownish spots above anal angle, sometimes centred with silver; costa marked with six or seven longitudinal brownish patches at intervals; outer margin narrowly, and inner margin conspicuously, margined with brown. Hind-wing pinkish salmon colour, pale golden yellow externally, veins on outer margin bright golden yellow; underside pale salmon colour, suffused with golden yellow; costa of forewing and hindwing obscurely barred with brown.—A.S.O.

CHRYSOPHANUS ERINUS, Fabricius.—(Plate XII., ♀, and Underside.)

Papilio erinus, Fabricius, Syst. Ent., p. 525 (1775); Donovan, Ins. New Holl., pl. 31, fig. 3 (1803).
Chrysophanus erinus, Olliff, Proc. Linn. Soc. N.S. Wales, x., p. 717 (1886).
Polyoyma enarytha, Scott, MS.

During the summer months we have frequently found these caterpillars feeding on the *Cassytha paniculata*, to the long tendrils of which they adhere by means of their viscous and slug-like bodies. When full grown they measure about 11 lines in length, are limaciform, slightly pubescent, and laciniate, with the back elevated, and head and feet minute. In some the colour throughout is of a beautiful pale green, in others the back is yellowish, each side edged by a row of small red spots, and with a conspicuous red patch at the anterior and posterior portions.

The chrysalis, in length nearly 7 lines, is of a light pinkish fawn colour, with several longitudinal rows of small black spots; the anterior portion bifurcate, the abdomen much compressed laterally, and broader than the thorax; dorsal portion ridged, and terminating in a sharp point. Attached by the tail, and girt by a silken medial band, with the head upwards. The female perfect insect attains to 1¼ inches in expanse; the male is slightly smaller.

The *Antennæ* ....(fig. 1, female) terminate in an elongated club, not grooved laterally.

The *Labial palpi* (fig. 2, female) large, second joint more than double the length of terminal; male, three times the length of terminal; in both slender and acuminated at the apex, and almost naked; basal joint small; this and the second moderately scaly and hairy; the whole projecting forwards and slightly upwards

The *Legs* ....with the anterior pair perfect in both sexes; second and posterior pairs (fig. 3) with two small spurs on tibiæ; tibiæ and tarsi, sparingly covered with scales, the latter also setigerous. Pulvilli large, claws minute.

The upper surface of the male is throughout of a shining purplish brown, deepening slightly towards the margins, with the cilia whitish; the female shining purplish blue, broadly margined with black. In both sexes the thorax, head, and abdomen are purplish brown. With respect to the under surface, both sexes are alike, being throughout of a light silvery grey; on the forewings two transverse rows of small indistinct brown patches, the two adjoining the anal angle large and black; two small marks on the exterior margin of the discoidal cell. The hindwings are occupied by numerous brownish patches.

Figures of the upper and under surface of the female butterfly, and the larva and chrysalis on the *Cassytha paniculata*, are given in the present illustration.

[*C. erinus* has been recorded from Bowen, Rockhampton, and Gayndah, in Queensland, and from various localities in Victoria, South Australia, and Tasmania.]

HOLOCHILA ABSIMILIS, Felder.—(Plate XII., ♂, ♀, and Underside.)

Holochila absimilis, Felder, Verh. Zool.-Bot. Ges. Wien, xii., p. 490 (1862); Reise Novara, Lep., ii., p. 261, pl. 32, fig. 14, 15 ♂, 16 ♀ (1865).
Polyoyma absimilis, Scott, MS.

This species is more common, and at the same time more beautiful, than the preceding one, the metallic lustre of the male showing to great advantage when the little creature darts with rapid wing around the tops of trees, ever and anon returning nearly to the same spot, and expanding its wings in the full enjoyment of the sunshine, very unlike the feeble and wavering movements of *Lampides alsulus* and *Lycæna bætica*.

The larva is limaciform, the body laciniate, the back slightly elevated; a lateral ridge in the region of the stigmata, projecting angularly near the posterior extremity, which is flattened and truncated; the first segment bifurcated, protruding beyond and hiding the minute black head. Generally the body is throughout a beautiful pale green, but an occasional specimen is met with of a dull fleshy tint. When full grown it measures 11 lines in length, is viscous, and like the preceding species exudes some matter highly attractive to ants, numbers of which may be seen crawling over and caressing the larvæ with their antennæ. We find these caterpillars most frequently on the tender shoots and leaves of the *Cupania anacardioides*, but they are also met with on *Wistaria consequana* and *Robinia hispida*, both imported plants.

The chrysalis is found with the head upwards, and is supported by the tail and a medial band; is about 7 lines in length, and of a pale pinkish brown powdered over with black; on each side of the abdomen a longitudinal row of four crimson spots; the head bifurcate, abdomen compressed, and a dorsal ridge which becomes tuberculated on the thorax.

The expanse of wings in the perfect insect is slightly under 1¼ inches.

The *Antennæ* ....are long, terminating in a somewhat fusiform club, not grooved laterally. (Fig. 1, male).

The *Labial palpi* (fig. 2, female) long, projecting upwards and forwards higher than the head; basal joint small, second joint twice as long as the terminal, which latter is somewhat obtuse at the apex; basal and second joints thickly, and terminal thinly, clothed with scales and a few short hairs. In male much smaller, projecting to about three-fourths of the eye.

The *Legs* .... with the anterior pair perfect (fig. 3, female), second and posterior pairs (fig. 4) with two minute apical spurs; tibiæ and tarsi covered with scales, the latter being also setigerous; pulvilli large, claws minute.

The upper surface of the male is of a shining smalt blue, deepening very slightly towards the marginal borders, which are fringed alternately with black and white. In the female the disc of each wing is white, merging into a dark bluish slate colour towards the base. The remaining portion of the forewings is silky black, of the hindwings bluish slate colour, darkening into neutral tint at the outer margin. The cilia greyish white; the head, thorax, and abdomen slaty blue. The underside of both sexes is silvery white, with several transverse rows of wavy black lines, a discoidal marking, and a few black spots scattered near the base of the hindwings.

The caterpillar and chrysalis are drawn on the *Cupania anacardioides* in flower, together with figures of both sexes in their perfect state.

[*I1. absimilis* ranges from Cape York, through New South Wales, into Gippsland.]

LAMPIDES ALSULUS, Herrich-Schäffer.—(Plate XII, Upper and Underside).

Lycæna alsulus, Herrich-Schäffer, Stett. Ent. Zeit., 1869, p. 75; Semper, Journ. Mus. Godeffroy, IV, p. 160 (1879).
Polyommatus frequens, Scott, MS.

This very common little butterfly is abundant nearly throughout the year, and in the neighbourhood of Sydney specimens may be seen even during the coldest months fluttering over the grass and weeds in gardens, or at the roadside. The larva feeds in the pods of the common pea and other leguminous plants, also on lucerne and various species of trefoil. It is onisciform, slightly pubescent, and of a pale green with a lateral stripe of darker colour, and slightly over 5 lines in length. The chrysalis is 4 lines in length, of a dark cream colour, with three abdominal rows of small spots, blunt in form, and is attached by the tail and a medial band. The perfect insect rarely exceeds 13 lines in expanse.

The *Antennæ* ....(fig. 1) are moderately long, clavate, and blunt at the tips, with a lateral groove.

The *Labial palpi* (fig. 2) project forwards and upwards to about the top of the eye; second joint four times longer than the basal, and half as long again as the terminal, which latter is pointed and nearly naked; basal and second joints covered with scales, and rather long hairs beneath.

The *Legs* ....anterior pair, in the male the tarsus is composed of a single joint, terminating in one claw; in the female, perfect; second and posterior pairs (fig. 3) with two small apical spurs on the tibiæ; tibiæ and tarsi closely covered with scales, and with a few setæ.

The upper surface is of a pale shining purplish blue, broadly bordered at the outer margins with brown. The underside is light silvery drab, with a brown crescent at the extremity of the discoidal cell; near the hind margin a transverse row of somewhat ocellated spots, and two wavy or scalloped bands; a few spots near the basal portion of the lower wings. The spots and markings are brown, faintly edged with white.

The plant figured is the *Indigofera australis*, upon which the larva and chrysalis are placed.

[*L. alsulus* is found throughout Australia and Tasmania, and extends to Fiji, Samoa, and the Philippines.]

LYCÆNA BÆTICA, Linnæus.—(Plate XII, ♂, ♀, and Underside.)

Papilio bæticus, Linnæus, Syst. Nat., i, p. 789 (1767).
Lycæna bætica, Horsfield, Cat. Lep. E.I.C. p. 80 (1829), Trimen, South African Butt., II, p. 58 (1887).
Papilio damoetes, Fabricius, Syst. Ent., p. 526 (1775); Donovan, Ins. New Holl., pl. 31, fig. 2 (1805); Trimen, loc. cit.
Lycæna leguminis, Scott, MS.
LIFE-HISTORY: Godart, Enc. Meth., ix, p. 653 (1819); Wollaston (Mrs. E.), Ann. Mag. Nat. Hist., 5 ser., iii, p. 324 (1879); Trimen, loc. cit.

The *L. bætica* is very widely distributed, its range extending from the south of Europe into India, Java, and Australia.* Here, as in the other countries mentioned, they are found in considerable abundance, disporting themselves in company with *Lampides alsulus*, or other small blues, over meadows and cultivated lands.

* [The species is now known to extend throughout Europe, Africa, and Asia, and is even found in the most remote oceanic islands, including Lord Howe Island and Norfolk Island; but up to this time, curiously enough, it does not appear to have been observed in New Zealand.—A.S.O.]

EXPLANATION OF PLATE X.

CŒQUOSA TRIANGULARIS, Donovan.

Larva and Variety.—Fig. 1, Pupa. Fig. 2, Portion of antenna of male. Fig. 3, Head, side-view showing palpi. Fig. 4, Foreleg of male. Fig. 5, Hindleg of female.

Food-plant: *Persoonia lanceolata*.

EXPLANATION OF PLATE XI.

OPHIDERES SALAMINIA, Cramer.
(OPHIDERES ATKINSONI, on plate).

Larva.—Fig. 1, Pupa. Fig. 2, Proboscis or modified maxillæ. Fig. 3, Head, side-view. Fig. 4, Labial palpus. Fig. 5, Foreleg. Fig. 6, Hindleg.

Food-plant: *Sarcopetalum harveyanum*.

CHARAGIA EXIMIA, Scott (Male).
(PHLOIOPSYCHE EXIMIA, on plate).

Larva and Burrow.—Fig. 1, Pupa. Fig. 2, Antenna. Figs. 3 and 4, Labial palpi. Fig. 5, Foreleg. Fig. 6, Hindleg.

Food-plant: *Dodonæa viscosa*.

EXPLANATION OF PLATE XII.

CHRYSOPHANUS ERINUS, Fabricius (Female).
(POLYCYMA CASSYTHÆ, on plate).

Larva and Pupa.—Fig. 1, Antenna. Fig. 2, Head and palpus, side-view. Fig. 3, Hindleg.

Food-plant: *Cassytha paniculata*.

The original coloured drawing by Helena Scott is at the Australian Museum and — not quite the same as this. The younger larva is reddish and also the seeds of the foodplant and the position of the butterflies is different. It must have been the basis of this lithograph. It bears a legend "Polyommatus hyacinthinus" over which has been pasted "Polycyma cassytha". I cannot find any reference to cassytha. G. Waterhouse 1941

HOLOCHILA ABSIMILIS, Felder (Male and Female).
(POLYCYMA ABSIMILIS, on plate).

Larva and Pupa.—Fig. 1, Antenna. Fig. 2, Head and palpus, side-view. Fig. 3, Foreleg of female. Fig. 4, Hindleg.

Food-plant: *Cupania anacardioides*.

LAMPIDES ALSULUS, Herrich-Schäffer.
(POLYOMMATUS PREQUENS, on plate).

Zizeeria labradus Godt.

Larva and Pupa.—Fig. 1, Antenna. Fig. 2, Head and palpus, side-view. Fig. 3, Hindleg.

Food-plant: *Indigofera australis*.

LYCÆNA BÆTICA, Linnæus (Male and Female).
(LYCÆNA LEGUMINIS, on plate).

Larva and Pupa.—Fig. 1, Antenna. Fig. 2, Head and palpus, side-view. Fig. 3, Hindleg.

Food-plant: *Swainsona galegifolia*.

The larva may be found on the common esculent pea, the *Colutea frutescens*, various species of *Dolichos*, *Lathyrus*, and other imported plants, and on the indigenous *Swainsona*, feeding in the interior of the seed pods, in which it undergoes its entire metamorphoses. It is about 6 lines in length, dull and sluggish in its movements, oniseiform, slightly pubescent, varying from pale green to a pinkish white, with a lateral row of small black dots, and several wavy dorsal lines. Head small, black.

The chrysalis is short and blunt in form, fastened by the tail and a medial band. The colour light brown, with a few rows of black dots on the abdomen.

The perfect insect measures about 1½ inches in expanse

The *Antennæ* ....(fig. 2). are moderately long and abruptly clavate, grooved laterally.

The *Labial palpi* (fig. 2), in the male, project upwards and forwards to nearly even with the top of the head; basal and terminal joints of an equal length, second joint three times longer; basal and second joints thickly covered with scales, and with rather long hairs beneath; terminal nearly naked; in the female the terminal joint is much longer than in the male, and slightly bent downwards towards the tip.

The *Legs* ....anterior pair, in the male, consist of a single joint, terminating in one claw; in the female, perfect; second and posterior pairs (fig. 3) with two small apical spurs on tibiæ; tibiæ and tarsi covered with scales, the latter also provided with rows of setæ.

The upper surface of the female, from the base to about the middle of the wings, is of a shining bluish lavender, changing gradually from pale to dark brown towards the exterior margins. On the lower wings, adjoining the outer margin, is a row of faint ocelli, the two at the anal angle large, with black centres and white irides. Beneath these proceeds a thin and graceful tail-like appendage of a black colour, tipped with white. In the male the upper surface presents more of the lavender hue, continued nearly to the outer margins, which are of a dark brown. Beneath both sexes are alike, the ground colour being of a shining white, suffused with drab towards the base, and thickly banded transversely on the inner half with fawn colour. Towards the outer margins white, bordered by a chain of white circular markings like indistinct ocelli, the two at the anal angles large, distinct, with black centres, innulated above with orange and beneath with silvery blue, resembling in miniature the eye on a peacock's tail. Abdomen and legs white.

The *Swainsona galegifolia*, formerly a very common plant on the Lower Hunter, is figured. A more showy species, *S. greyana*, is known as the Poison Pea of the River Darling, from its fatally injurious effect when eaten by sheep, horses, and other stock. Both these plants afford food for the larvæ of *Lycæna bætica* in certain localities.

ANTHERÆA ASTROPHELA, Walker.—(Plate XIII. ♂ and ♀).

Antheræa astrophela, Walker, Cat. Lep. Ilet. Brit. Mus., V., p. 1235 (1855); ♀.
Antheræa simplex, Walker, loc. cit. p. 1236, ♂. Scott, MS.

This pretty species of Antheræa first came under our notice many years ago, at Ash Island on the Lower Hunter River, where the fine forest trees upon which the larvæ fed—the native ash (*Elœocarpus obcatus*) and native pine (*Podocarpus elata*) of the early settlers—existed in considerable numbers, and afforded much valuable timber. Indeed so common then was this insect that we have seen the cocoons attached in such numbers to the twigs of the "Fustic"—*Cudrania javanensis*—and other shrubs in the vicinity of their feeding grounds, that a good-sized bag or basket might have been quickly filled without entailing much labour on the part of the collector, each twig or stem carrying one or more of the odd-looking brown excrescences, in some cases built one on top of the other in a fashion embarrassing, to say the least, to the occupant of the undermost tenement. The mature caterpillars must occasionally wander far afield in search of a final resting place, as we have found the cocoons attached to orange, quince, pomegranate, and other orchard trees, at considerable distances from their proper food-plants.

It has sometimes occurred to us that the plump chrysalids of this Antheræa may have afforded in times past a succulent and welcome addition to the not well supplied larder of the Australian savage, as on sundry occasions when we have availed ourselves in our entomological walks of the help of the few, and now, alas, degenerate descendants of the native tribes who still lingered around their old hunting grounds on the islands of the Lower Hunter, we were frequently presented by them with handfuls of the cocoons, accompanied by many significant signs that they were "good to eat."

There are two broods of this Antheræa produced during the spring and summer months, the finest and brightest specimens being captured in January and February, when they may be seen any fine afternoon in company with a larger and more showy species, *Antheræa janetta*, for at least an hour before sunset, flying about in a rapid but uncertain fashion, blundering against obstacles in their path, then recovering themselves and resuming their flight in great haste—the males at such times, owing to their bright yellow colour, being much more conspicuous than their duller-hued consorts.

They usually rest with the wings placed horizontally.

The eggs are produced in large numbers and are greyish white, compressed oval in form, and are attached to the plant either singly or in clusters of two or three.

The young larvæ at first are blackish, with segmental whorls of hair, which, after their first change of skin, develop into small tubercles. Occasionally the black colour is replaced by a dull greenish-yellow, but as a rule the full grown caterpillar, which is 2½ inches long, is throughout velvety-black, with six well defined equidistant parallel bands of light green running from the third to the antepenultimate segment. Springing from the centre of these bands and on each segment (with the exception of the anterior and the last two) are six white tubercles, of a bright yellow ringed with scarlet at their bases, and surmounted with symmetrical clusters of white hair. On the two posterior segments the tubercles are only four in number, of slightly larger size, and tinged with yellow, while they are quite absent on the anterior segment where they are replaced by hair. A thin fringe of stiff white hair is placed between each segment, and there is also a lateral bordering of short hair over the legs, which, with the head and extremity are dull red.

Towards the end of October and again in March the cocoons are spun, being attached lengthways to the stem; they are coriaceous, oval, and dark brown in colour.

The chrysalis (fig. 1) is shining blackish red, about 1 inch long, and half an inch wide. The moth, like the *Antheræa eucalypti* described in the first part of this work (Vol. I., p. 2), emerges from its cocoon by moistening one extremity with a fluid which is secreted for the purpose, rotating its body, and ripping open the envelope by means of the strong curved hooks placed on each shoulder.

The *Antennæ* ....in both sexes four-pectinated on each joint; the pectinations in the male being very long, and much developed, each pectination finely ciliated at the sides; the antennæ (figs. 2 and 3) are broadest in the middle, and from thence the pectinations gradually decrease in length towards both extremities.

The *Labial palpi* (figs. 4, 5, and 6) three-jointed, small, but distinct, and bent downwards in front of the mouth; terminal joint round at tip, rather more than one-third the length of second, which is nearly double that of the basal. The whole are hairy and scaly, the hairs thickest on the outer portion.

The *Maxillæ* ....obsolete.

The *Legs*: ....the anterior pair (fig. 7) spurless and much more pilose than the others; second and posterior pairs (figs. 8 and 9) with two small spurs on the tibiæ. In the male the tibiæ and tarsi very densely clothed with hairs; the tarsi five-jointed, barely as long as the tibiæ, the terminal joint elongated, and terminating in a pair of small claws. Femora densely pilose. Female much less pilose than male and joints therefore more distinct.

In outline the male of the *Antheræa astrophela* has not got the graceful curves of its congeners the *Antheræa eucalypti*, *A. helena*, or *A. janetta*, the upper wings being shorter and more rounded. Its colour is also more uniform, being as a rule throughout pale clear chrome yellow, slightly salmon at the tips, which are much crumpled between the veins. A distinct band of purplish black is placed transversely on both wings, and there are two short additional bars on the inner angle of the upper wing. An ocellus ringed with purplish black, lunulated with red and white, and with a small hyaline pupil, occupies the centre of each wing; costa and patagia dark grey; abdomen, head, and antennæ yellow. The female is throughout pinkish brown, with the transverse bands, ocelli, costa, and patagia similar in colour to the male, but darker and richer in hue. The male measures 4 inches in expanse, the female 4½ inches.

The caterpillar is figured on the native pine, *Podocarpus elata*, and the cocoon attached to another characteristic indigenous tree, the *Acronychia lævis*, both plants bearing fruits much appreciated by the wild pigeons, opossums, etc., but otherwise valueless from an economic point of view. In a future number we hope to give the life-history of *Antheræa janetta*.

NETROCORYNE REPANDA, Felder. —(Plate XIV., 4).

Netrocoryne repanda, Felder, Reise Novara, Lep., III., p. 507, pl. lxx., fig. 10 (1867); cf. Phæz, Berl. Ent. Zeit., XXVI., p. 76 (1882).
Ismilda calpeuda, Prittwitz, Stett. Ent. Zeit., p. 187, pl. iv., fig. 2, a b (1868).
Hesperia curvha, Scott, MS.
Larva history Mathew, Trans. Ent. Soc. Lond., 1888, p. 181.

We originally discovered the habitations of this pretty species of Netrocoryne in considerable numbers at Ash Island, commonly on the *Nephelium leiocarpum*, and occasionally on the *Scolopia Brownii*, the *Notolea longifolia*, and *Podocarpus elata*, but subsequently we have found them inhabiting similar trees and shrubs in the Botanic and many private gardens in or about Sydney, having probably accompanied their food plants (some of which are highly ornamental) to the new localities selected for them. Like most of the Hesperiidæ, the larva of Netrocoryne shelters itself during life beneath a leafy covering, the form of which however, alters materially during the progress from infancy to maturity. When but a few days old the infant larva cuts a small and perfectly circular piece, about the size of a pea, from the leaf, and attaches it with silken threads to the upper surface of the same or another leaf, thus forming a secure habitation under which it dwells, and from whence it issues in search of food, by a small aperture at the upper end. As the increasing size of the larva demands more roomy accommodation, larger pieces of the leaf are cut out and similarly attached, the old dwellings being then deserted, and as they soon become brown and shrivelled they impart to the tree in time a somewhat diseased appearance. When almost mature the larva selects a larger leaf, and cutting out a sufficient portion to comfortably cover its body, secures this to a fresh leaf, and, when the time for the change to the chrysalis approaches, further provides for its security and comfort by lining this habitation with finely spun web, which is also carried up the leaflet to the main stalk, thus preventing the nest from falling off or being blown from the tree by the wind.

The full grown larva is 1¼ inch in length, cylindrical, and very plump in form. The head is black and rough ; the two first thoracic segments (which can be protruded at times until they apparently attenuate) are clear bright yellow, with a small lateral spot of rich black on the first, and two similar spots on the second segment ; the two posterior segments are also bright yellow with similar black spots. The whole of the intermediate segments are on the upper portion a clear bluish-slate colour, with five broad longitudinal rich black bands (slightly disconnected on the third thoracic segment) one occupying the centre of the back, and two on each side. A yellow line, in which are placed the black stigmata, passes immediately over the legs, which, with the abdominal portions, are pale greenish white ; feet black.

The chrysalis (fig. 1) is nearly ⅞ inch in length with slightly projecting angles on the shoulders and beneath the head, and the trunk projecting ; the abdomen sharply pointed and secured to the silken lining of the nest. The head and wing cases are rich deep purple, the abdomen lavender, thickly dusted with whitish bloom.'

The *Antennæ* ....(fig. 2) are rather long and clavate, the club, gradually attenuating to the apex, and curving, forms a hook.

The *Labial palpi* (fig. 3 and 4) project forwards ; are pilose underneath, scaly above ; the basal joint short, the second very long, slightly curved, the third or apical joint bent slightly downwards.

The *Legs* : ....tibiæ of the anterior pair very pilose, spurless ; of the second pair with short hair and two spurs at each of the apices ; of the posterior pair (fig. 5) with tufts of long hair at the base, the remaining portion hairy, with four spurs, two at the apices, and two at the middle. Tarsi of the whole five-jointed ; first joint equal in length to the remainder, hairy, and terminated by small claws.

The expanse of the perfect insect is about 2 inches.

The wings are horizontal in repose, and the insect is diurnal. The entire upper surface is rich golden brown, relieved on the anterior wings by an irregular broad transverse patch of pale yellowish white, interrupted by the nervures, and which in many instances extends over the costa and becomes shining yellow. Near the top of the wing are three small spots, somewhat triangular in form, and on the middle of the lower wing an oval spot, also yellowish white. All these patches and spots are diaphanous, and strongly relieved by an edging of black. A wavy line of small black spots passes across the centre of the lower wing, and a blackish brown fringe surrounds the whole external margin. The wings are rather triangular, with the outer margins broken by wide shallow denticulations, and so produced posteriorly as to be subemulate.

The under surface of the insect is similar in colour to the upper, but lighter in hue.

The plate represents the larva, with its leafy dwelling ; one of its food plants, the *Nephelium leiocarpum*, in flower and fruit ; and the perfect insect.

PAMPHILA PHINEUS, Cramer.—(Plate XIV., ♂ and ♀).

Papilio phineus, Cramer, Pap. Exot., II., p. 123, pl. clxxvi. E (1779).
Hesperia phineus, Latreille, Enc. Meth., IX., p. 763, No. 107 (1823).
Pamphila palmarum, Scott, MS.
LIFE-HISTORY : Mathew, Trans. Ent. Soc. Lond., 1888, p. 179.

Previous to the acclimatization of the date and other foreign palms, we usually found the caterpillars of this showy Pamphila feeding, both at Sydney and the Hunter River, upon the fronds of the indigenous palms, *Livistona australis* or "Cabbage Tree" of the early settlers, and *Ptychosperma elegans* "Bangala Palm," although occasionally we have seen a stray

---

* [Mr. G. F. Mathew, who found this species feeding on *Eugenia*, remarks that the chrysalis is attached by the anal extremity and encircled by a silken girdle.]

specimen inhabiting the common reed, *Phragmites communis*. As the species now under consideration is of very common occurrence, the graceful foliage of the Palms suffer greatly by its ravages, the folded leaflets being welded together in every direction to form the habitations of the caterpillars, who issue thence and devour all the leaflets in their immediate vicinity, and thus in time impart a ragged and dishevelled appearance to the previously symmetrical leaf. The full grown caterpillar measures about 1¾ inches, and is throughout of a very delicate transparent bluish green, with two conspicuous yellow spots on the ninth segment, and yellow stigmata. The body is attenuated; the head large, horny, and fawn-coloured, with black markings, and during repose placed even with the body; the tail flat, and fringed with fine whitish hair. Previous to the transformation to the chrysalis, the caterpillar strengthens the silken webbing and closes the aperture of its dwelling.

The chrysalis (fig. 1) is 1 inch in length, delicate greenish white in colour, dusted with a powdery substance,* and of slender form; two small black spots are placed obliquely on each side of each abdominal segment, and the abdomen and head are both furnished with reddish cilia.

The *Antennæ* ....(fig. 2) long, clavate, and strongly hooked at the extremity.

The *Labial palpi* (figs. 3, 4, and 5) robust, projecting upwards a little beyond the tops of the eyes; three-jointed, second joint twice the length of the basal, and both densely clothed with thick hairs; terminal short, obtuse, and covered with hairs.

The *Legs:* ....anterior pair spurless; second pair with two spurs, and posterior pair (fig. 6) with spurs on middle and apex of tibiæ. Tarsi five jointed, with long scales and bristles beneath, terminated by two claws, each having a long hair above; pulvilli small.

The perfect insect is diurnal, and like the other members of this group, rapid and erratic in its movements; it rests either with all the wings elevated, or with the upper pair elevated and the lower horizontal.

The upper surface of the female is throughout rich bronze brown, and across the centre of both wings, commencing at the inner margin and running towards the tips, is a band of dull yellow, formed into spots or patches by the nervures; and also two subcostal dull yellow patches on the upper wings; the marginal fringe is dull yellow. Abdomen and head robust, dark brown, with yellowish hair.

The upper surface of the male is also rich dark brown, but the dull yellow spots and markings of the female are here replaced by continuous but irregular transverse bands of golden yellow, and the marginal fringe is also golden yellow. Head, thorax, and abdomen shining golden brown.

A small portion of the frond or leaf, the flower spathe and ripe seeds of *Livistona australis* are shown on the plate; also the caterpillar and both sexes of the perfect insect.

AGARISTA LEWINI, Boisduval. (Plate XV.)

Agarista Lewinii, Boisduval, Voy. de l'Astrolabe, Ent., p. 176 (1832).
LIFE-HISTORY: McCoy, Prod. Zool. of Victoria, I., p. 27 (1878).

As yet we have only found this Agarista in its larval state, at Ash Island, where from September to March it was tolerably abundant on the *Epilobium junceum* and the imported Œnotheras. The presence, however, of the imago in many other localities, proves that its range must be considerable.†

When mature the larva measures about 1½ inches, and is throughout very pale yellow; the first three segments have on their anterior edges a series of short irregular black bands, and also some delicate pencillings of black; the remaining segments are occupied with numerous irregular black transverse bands, terminating above the stigmata, which are each encircled by a black ring connected below with a comma-shaped black marking. The whole pattern bears a resemblance to Chinese characters. On the penultimate segment is a connected row of slightly raised spots of bright orange red; the head and upper portion of the first segment is also orange slightly marked with black, and there is a patch of the same colour over the caudal feet; thoracic feet black, legs pale yellow; a whorl of fine whitish hairs proceeds from each segment.

---

* [Mr. Mathew states that this powdery matter exudes from beneath the ninth, tenth, and eleventh segments of the larva as it lies quiescent before its change to the pupa state. He also observed that the eggs are globular, shining, and pale greenish yellow in colour.]

† [In the summer of 1866, I found a healthy brood of the larvæ at Menindie, Darling River, feeding on the common Balsam.—H.F.]

AND THEIR TRANSFORMATIONS.   15

The cocoon is formed of agglutinated particles of earth, and is placed near the surface of the ground. The chrysalis (fig. 1) is ⅜ inch in length, and throughout dark brown, of somewhat attenuated form, the extremity truncated. The perfect insect measures slightly over 2 inches.

The *Antennæ* ....(fig. 2) thin and long, gradually and slightly thickening towards the middle, then tapering to a point.

The *Labial palpi* (figs. 3 and 4) three-jointed; basal and middle joints nearly equal, covered with scales, and bunches of long hairs underneath; terminal joint about half the length of preceding and nearly smooth; the whole projecting forwards.

The *Legs:* ....anterior pair spurless; second with two spurs; posterior pair (fig. 5) with four spurs, two at apex and two on middle tibiæ. Tibiæ and tarsi clothed with hair-like scales, the former with long tufts of hairs on the anterior portions. Tarsi five-jointed, with rows of small setæ internally, and terminated by small claws.

The colour of the entire upper surface is velvety jet black with several transverse bands or patches of pale straw colour on the upper wings, the outer one being much the largest; close to, and parallel with, the outer margin, is a double row of short longitudinal straw-coloured lines. In most instances the lower wings have no markings, but in some specimens, as in the one depicted, there is a distinct transverse spot or patch in the centre. Marginal fringe of upper wings black, with white at tips and anal angles; of lower wings alternately black and white. Thorax and abdomen black; the former with longitudinal bands of straw colour, the latter with a lateral row of small yellowish spots, and tufted posteriorly with vermilion-coloured hairs.

The larva, with its food plant *Epilobium junceum*, and the perfect insect, are figured in the plate.

Professor McCoy states that the *Agarista Lewini* is not uncommon near Melbourne, the larva feeding on the *Epilobium tetragonum*, which is an abundant weed. The figures given in his illustration, both of the larva and imago, are very much inferior in size to those bred by us in New South Wales.

AGARISTA GLYCINÆ, Lewis.—(Plate XV.)

Phalænoides glycinæ, Lewin, Nat. Hist. Lep. Ins. N.S. Wales, p. 2, pl. i. (1805).
Agarista glycinæ, Boisduval, Voy. de l'Astrolabe, Ent., 175; Spéc. Gén. Lép., 1, pl. xiv., fig. 3; Guérin, Icon. Règn. Anim., Ins., pl. lxxxiii., fig. 2.
LIFE-HISTORY: Lewin, *loc. cit.*; McCoy, Prod. Zool. Victoria. I., p. 30 (1878).

It is evident, from the observation cursorily made by Lewin in 1805, that the caterpillars of this Agarista "feed sometimes on the grape vine," that they had not then developed the destructive characters which they have since assumed, and which fairly entitle them to a foremost place in the list of pests dangerous to the viticulturist. They enjoy immunity from birds, either owing to the acrid greenish juice which they eject from their mouths when alarmed, or from some other protective influence, and thus small armies carry on their work of destruction in the vineyard until scarcely a whole leaf is left. Nor are their ravages confined to the grape vine, as many of the introduced species of Vitis and Cissus, the Virginia Creeper, &c., are completely destroyed by them.

When full grown the female larva measures 2 inches; the ground colour is very pale creamy-white, relieved by numerous irregular annular black lines and spots, forming an intricate but symmetrical pattern divided down the centre of the back, and bordered on each side by a narrow but distinct whitish horizontal band. On the penultimate segment are four conspicuous and slightly protuberant deep crimson spots of graduated size; the stigmata, with the exception of those near the head, are also deep crimson; and beneath these, over the legs, are shining ochreous spots, connected with each other by a line of irregular spots of pale gamboge yellow. Head and upper part of first segment shining ochre, with several black divisions or markings; feet and legs large, shining ochre, with black tips; whorls of fine whitish hair on each segment. In some specimens there is an additional row of small crimson spots over the stigmata, but this may be a sexual distinction.

The cocoon, like that of the preceding species, is found under the surface of the ground, and is composed of agglutinated earth. The chrysalis (fig. 1) is about ⅞ inch in length, dark brown throughout, of somewhat attenuated form, and slightly truncated at the extremity.

The perfect female insect measures 2¼ inches; the male is much smaller.

The *Antennæ* ....(fig. 2) slightly thickened towards the middle and terminated in a point, neither arcuated nor hooked.

The *Labial palpi* (figs. 3 and 4) are three-jointed; basal and second joints nearly equal in length, and covered with scales and hairs; terminal joint rather shorter than either, somewhat cylindrical, and covered with a few short hairs; the whole projecting forwards.

The *Legs*: ....anterior pair spurless; second pair (fig. 5) with two spurs at apex of tibiæ; posterior pair with four spurs, two on middle and two on apex of tibiæ; tarsi five-jointed and terminating in two small claws. Tibiæ and tarsi covered with feathery scales, the former of which are furnished exteriorly with a tuft of long hairs.

Wings decumbent in repose; insect diurnal. The upper surface of both sexes is throughout rich velvety black, with two broad wavy pale yellow transverse bands on the superior wings, the outer one extending nearly across the middle of each wing; several narrow and rather indistinct bars occupy the base, and near the outer margins are several short whitish lines, indicating the nervures, and also a short subcostal bar. Marginal fringe of upper wings black, with white at tips and anal angles; of lower wings white, with deep black scallops. Thorax black, with longitudinal streaks of pale greenish white; abdomen tufted with vermilion coloured hairs. The under surface is similar to above, but presents additionally two wavy transverse whitish bands towards the middle of inferior wings, and a whitish costal streak. The abdomen is also ringed with vermilion hairs, and the legs tufted with the same colour.

The circular spots on the lower wings, mentioned by Lewin as exclusively belonging to the males, are rarely met with, and then are merely a varietal difference, certainly not a sexual distinction.

We have seen the larvæ feeding indifferently on the various species of Cissus and Vitis, the Œnotheras and Balsams, and on *Hardenbergia monophylla*, the plant figured in the illustration in conjunction with the larva and perfect insect.* The grape vine, however, seems to constitute its general and apparently most congenial food.

AGARISTA DONOVANI, Boisduval.—(Plate XV.)

Agarista Donovani, Boisduval, Voy. de l'Astrolabe, Ent., p. 176 (1832).

This species is also not commonly met with in the larval state, although fairly abundant in the perfect form. We have as yet only found it on the *Vitis antarctica*, but it probably feeds, like its congeners, on many allied plants. It measures 1¾ inch; the ground colour is bistre brown, with a broadish annular band of white on each segment, bearing in the centre a row of raised black spots, each emitting a thin white hair. Head black; feet and legs blackish brown.

The cocoon in form, material, and situation, exactly resembles those of the preceding species. The chrysalis (fig. 1) is slightly over ¾ inch in length, reddish brown in colour, slim in form, and truncated posteriorly.

The female perfect insect measures about 2 inches; male smaller.

---

* [Professor McCoy states that before the introduction of the vine into Victoria, the larvæ of *Agarista Lewini* fed on *Gnaphalium luteoalbum*].

The *Antennæ* ....(fig. 2) gradually thickened towards the tip, which is somewhat obtuse.

The *Labial palpi* (figs. 3 and 4) three-jointed, basal and second joints nearly equal in length, scaly, with long hairs beneath; terminal joint shorter, obtuse at the tip, and clothed with scales.

The *Legs:* ....anterior pair spurless; second pair with two spurs at apex of tibiæ; posterior pair (fig. 5) with four spurs, two at apex, two on middle of tibiæ. Tibiæ and tarsi scaly, the former with tufts of long hair anteriorly.

Upper surface of perfect insect shining jet black, with numerous scattered pale yellowish patches on outer half of upper wings, and two longitudinal streaks of yellowish white near the base. Across the centre of lower wings is an irregular broad transverse bar of pale yellow, much indented at the borders. Marginal fringes alternately black and white. Thorax and abdomen, head and antennæ, black, with a few faint yellowish transverse lines on thorax, and annular rings of straw colour on abdomen, which is tufted with vermilion and black hairs.

The *Vitis antarctica* in flower and fruit, the larva, and the perfect insect are figured on the plate.

AGARISTA LATINA. Donovan.—(Plate XV.)

Phalæna latinus, Donovan, Nat. Hist. Ins. New Holl., pl. xxxii. (1805).

Agarista latinus, Boisduval, Voy. de l'Astrolabe, Ent., 174.

This is by no means a common species, and although we have occasionally seen the perfect insect both near Sydney, and at Ash Island on the Hunter River, we have never obtained the larvæ except at the former place, where they were captured near the Botanic Gardens, feeding on the *Haloragis teucrioides*. At first sight they might easily be mistaken for the *Agarista glycine*, from which they differ very little in general appearance; but they are smaller, measuring when full grown about 1¼ inches. The ground colour is pale yellow, covered, down to the space over the stigmata, with numerous short fine annular black lines. On the penultimate segment are four conspicuous slightly raised patches or spots of dark crimson; and a lateral row of spots, one on each segment, extends from the head to the eleventh segment, the one on the tenth segment being crimson, the remainder orange yellow. A connected series of patches of gamboge yellow runs above the feet, and, on the last segment are a few annular yellow patches; head and feet orange red; fine whitish hairs encircle each segment.

The cocoon resembles those made by the species already described. The chrysalis (fig. 7) measures ⅞ inch, and is throughout dark reddish brown.

In expanse the perfect insect is slightly under 1⅜ inches.

The *Antennæ* ....(fig. 2) are filiform, and rather obtuse at the tips.

The *Labial palpi* (figs. 3 and 4) are three-jointed; basal and middle joints nearly equal in length, and densely clothed with scales and long hairs; apical joint smaller, and nearly naked. The whole projecting forwards and slightly upwards.

The *Legs:* ....anterior pair (fig. 5) spurless; second pair with two spurs; posterior pair with four spurs, two on middle and two at apex of tibiæ. The tibiæ are tufted with long hairs externally. Tarsi five-jointed, hairy, and terminated by two small claws.

Wings decumbent in repose; insect diurnal. The upper surface of both wings is shining jet black, with a broad irregular band of yellow, extending right across the centre, on the upper wings; this band becomes white on the costal portion. Between this and the outer margin is a row, marking the nervures, of short white lines, and a few transverse white bands near the base of the wings. The lower wing has a deeply scalloped white border enclosing, near the anal angle, some black spots. Marginal fringe of upper wing black, with white at tip and anal angle; of lower wing, white. Thorax and head black, with numerous narrow white transverse bands across the shoulders; abdomen black, tufted with orange yellow.

It will be observed that the hairs on the bodies of the caterpillars of the four species of Agarista now given, are very unlike those of *Agarista agricola* and *A. casuarinæ*; they are not spatulate at the tips, nor do they possess a metallic lustre.

The perfect insect, and the caterpillar on the *Haloragis teucrioides*, form the plate.

EXPLANATION OF PLATE XIII.

ANTHERÆA ASTROPHELA, Walker (Male and Female).

(ANTHERÆA SIMPLEX, on plate).

Larva and Cocoon.—Fig. 1, Pupa. Fig. 2, Antenna of female. Fig. 3, Portion of same, much enlarged. Fig. 4, Head, palpus and portion of antenna, side-view. Figs. 5 and 6, Labial palpus. Figs. 7, 8 and 9, Fore, intermediate and hindlegs.

Food-plants : *Podocarpus elata* and *Acronychia laevis*.

Australian Lepidoptera
Plate 13

Antheraea simplex

EXPLANATION OF PLATE XIV.

NETHOCORYNE REPANDA, Felder (Female).

(HESPERIA COREBBA, on plate).

Larva and Shelter.—Fig. 1, Pupa. Fig. 2, Antenna. Fig. 3, Head and palpus, side-view. Fig. 4, Labial palpus. Fig. 5, Hindleg.

Food-plant: *Nephelium leiocarpum*.

---o---

PAMPHILA PHINEUS, Cramer (Male and Female).

(PAMPHILA PALMARUM, on plate).

Larva.—Fig. 1, Pupa. Fig. 2, Antenna. Fig. 3, Head and palpus, side-view. Fig. 4, Head and palpi, viewed from the front. Fig. 5, Labial palpus. Fig. 6, Hindleg.

Food-plant: *Livistona australis*.

EXPLANATION OF PLATE XV.

AGARISTA LEWINI, Boisduval.

Larva.—Fig. 1, Pupa. Fig. 2, Portion of antenna. Fig. 3, Head and palpus, side-view. Fig. 4, Labial palpus. Fig. 5, Hindleg.

Food-plant: *Epilobium junceum*.

---o---

AGARISTA GLYCINÆ, Lewin.

Larva.—Fig. 1, Pupa. Fig. 2, Portion of antenna. Fig. 3, Head and palpus, side-view. Fig. 4, Labial palpus. Fig. 5, Hindleg.

Food-plant: *Hardenbergia monophylla*.

---o---

AGARISTA DONOVANI, Boisduval.

Larva.—Fig. 1, Pupa. Fig. 2, Portion of antenna. Fig. 3, Head and palpus, side-view. Fig. 4, Labial palpus. Fig. 5, Hindleg.

Food-plant: *Vitis antarctica*.

---o---

AGARISTA LATINA, Donovan.

Larva.—Fig. 1, Pupa. Fig. 2, Portion of antenna. Fig. 3, Head and palpus, side-view. Fig. 4, Labial palpus. Fig. 5, Hindleg.

Food-plant: *Haloragis tenuicoides*.

PAPILIO ANACTUS, MACLEAY.—(Plate XVI., ♀).

Papilio anactus, W. S. Macleay, King's Surv. Austr., II., App. p. 458 (1827); Boisduval, Spec. Gén., I., p. 219 (1836); Westwood, Arcana Ent., II., pl. lii., fig. 5 (1843).

LIFE-HISTORY: Mathew, Trans. Ent. Soc. London, 1888, p. 176, pl. vi., fig. 2.

This well-known *Papilio* is tolerably common during the summer months about Sydney and its environs, and at the Hunter River, although not such a familiar object in our gardens as the showy *Papilio erectheus*, Don. There can be no doubt that, before the introduction of the orange and lemon into New South Wales, the caterpillars of *Papilio anactus* must have subsisted upon some indigenous tree, probably the native Lime or some allied plant, but personally, except on one occasion, we have always found them upon the Orange and Lemon trees—the exception alluded to being the capture of a fine full grown caterpillar feeding on the common Rue (*Ruta graveolens*), a plant, we may here mention, also favoured by *Papilio erectheus*. In its earliest stages the young larva of *Papilio anactus* closely resembles the young larva of *Papilio erectheus*, with which it may occasionally be seen in company, feeding on the Citron leaves; but a marked divergence occurs as it increases in size, as the yellow patches on each segment which distinguish it from *Papilio erectheus* soon make their appearance. These yellow patches are retained to maturity, when the caterpillar measures from 1¼ to 2 inches in length, the female being decidedly larger than the male; both sexes are cylindrical and plump in form, very dark bistre-brown throughout, finely punctured with white and blue dots; with three rows of conspicuous yellow spots or patches, one dorsal and the others lateral, running down the body from head to tail; a row of small spines, each rising from a small blue tubercle, springs from each segment between the dorsal and lateral yellow spots; and a row of white spots—in some specimens almost appearing as an undulating white line—is placed over the feet, which are brown with yellowish white markings; head shining brown with a white V-shaped mark. They are voracious feeders, and sluggish in habit, but if alarmed, like all the *Papilio* larvæ will protrude the retractile tentacula.

The chrysalis is about 1¼ inch in length, attached by the tail and a median band, with the head upwards; much produced and bifurcate in front above the eyes, with numerous small tubercular projections on the back and near the wing-covers; the ground colour is greyish, tinted in places with pale pink and green, and finely speckled and striated with darker brown or black.

In expanse the female perfect insect measures rather less than 3½ inches; the male about 3¼ inches.

The *Antennæ* ....(fig. 1) terminate in a gradual club, which is rounded at the apex and not compressed or grooved.

The *Labial palpi* (figs. 2 and 3) very small, hairy, scarcely projecting beyond the head; basal joint about twice the length of second; terminal about half the length of second, and rather globular in shape.

The *Legs* : ....long, slender, and almost devoid of scales or hair, but with several rows of short setæ on all the joints; anterior pair spurless; intermediate and posterior pairs (fig. 4) with two small spurs at their apices; tarsi terminating in strong claws.

Wings erect in repose.

The ground colour of both wings is jet black. In the discoidal cell, and between the nervules of the upper wing, are large oblong patches of an ashy or blackish-grey tint, and a row of oval white spots, close to the outer margin. The centre of the lower wing is white, with the discoidal cell and nervules distinctly outlined in black; five conspicuous crescentic patches of vermilion-red commence at the anal angle and run parallel with the outer margin, and above these are smaller patches of shining bluish scales, and two small white spots near the outer angle; margins of both wings alternately black and white; the lower wing with the denticulations somewhat produced, like a rudimentary tail. Head and thorax black, with yellowish hairs near base of antenna and in front, and a girdle of small white spots on the collar; two yellowish spots on thorax, and on base of abdomen; abdomen black in centre, and partly ringed with yellow and black at sides and extremity.

The under side is very similar to upper, but the patches are lighter in colour and larger. The sexes are alike in colouring.

The female caterpillar, chrysalis, and female butterfly, are figured on the orange (*Citrus aurantium*).

EUPLŒA CORINNA, Macleay.—(Plate XVI.)

Danais corinna, W. S. Macleay, King's Survey Austr., II., App., p. 402 (1827).

Chanapa corinna, Moore, Proc. Zool. Soc. London, XIV., p. 299 (1878).

Euploea angasii, Felder, Reise Novara, Lep., p. 343 (1867); Herrich-Schaffer, Stett. Ent., Zeit., p. 69, pl. ii., fig. 7 (1869); Exot. Schmett, II., fig. 108 (1869).

LIFE-HISTORY: H. Edwards, Victorian Naturalist, June, 1890, p. 4 (Pupa only).

We discovered some nearly full grown specimens of this showy caterpillar in March, at Ash Island, Hunter River, feeding upon the *Marsdenia suaveolens*, a pretty climbing plant of the group Asclepiadeæ.* When mature the larva measures 2¼ inches in length. It is smooth, cylindrical, and very slightly attenuated at both extremities; the ground colour as far as the stigmata is shining saturnine-yellow, closely covered with regular transverse black bands, and relieved occasionally with white on the middle of the segments; the abdominal portion beneath the stigmata is rich black, with a conspicuous white spot on each segment, the spots over the abdominal feet largest, and each having beneath a small band of saturnine-red. Springing from near the centre of the back, on the second, third, fifth, and eleventh segments, are pairs of long, thin, flexible black appendages, those on the second and third segment bending forwards, and measuring ¾ inch in length; those on the fifth segment curving gracefully at the tips; and those on the eleventh segment projecting backwards, somewhat curved and a little shorter; head black, with two white divisional markings. The favourite position of the caterpillar when at rest is with the anterior segments elevated and curved, as shown in the plate; when alarmed it exudes from its mouth a clear greenish fluid.

The chrysalis is suspended by the tail, is barely 1 inch in length, and is proportionately broad; the abdominal portion somewhat swollen, and the back of the thorax indented. The entire surface is brilliantly metallic, and reflects external objects with the fidelity of a mirror, and in different lights it assumes lovely opaline tints, utterly impossible to represent with the brush. Our butterflies took wing in April, but as is the case with many of the Danaids, an occasional specimen may be seen flying about in the winter months.

In expanse it measures 3⅞ inches.

The *Antennæ* ....(fig. 1) thicken very slightly towards the point, which is rather blunt.

The *Labial palpi* (fig. 2), rather large, projecting almost as far as the top of the eyes, and thickly covered with elongated scales; middle joint at least three times as long as basal (fig. 3), terminal joint not quite as long as basal, and blunt at apex.

The *Legs* ....the anterior pair (fig. 4) small and rudimentary, the tarsus being composed of one club-shaped articulation, with several pairs of small hooks at the extremity; the whole covered with scales. The intermediate and posterior pairs (fig. 5) long, slender, almost naked, with rows of small setæ beneath, and with two small spurs at the apices of tibiæ.

The wings are erect in repose.

The whole upper surface is silky brownish-black, with a row of large creamy-white irregular patches towards the outer margins of both wings, on the lower wing they are deeply denticulate and are arranged in an almost straight line to the anal angle; a row of white spots follow the outline of the margins, and on the costa and discoidal cell of upper wing are a few scattered white spots, while a short silvery semi-diaphanous streak is placed not far from the base of the upper wing, near the disc; head blackish-brown, with rows of small white spots on front, between the eyes, and on the collar; abdomen blackish-brown; margins whitish. The under surface is bronze-brown, darkest in the centre of upper wing, with markings disposed as above, but on the disc of the lower wing are several additional small white spots, and there are numerous white spots on the chest above the legs; palpi and legs black and white; abdomen banded with creamy-white.

The caterpillar, chrysalis, and upper and under views of the butterfly are given, with *Marsdenia suaveolens* in flower and seed.

---

*[In February, 1890, I observed a female *Euploea corinna* depositing her eggs on the young leaves of a vine of *Mandevilla suaveolens*, growing near Darling Point, Sydney. The eggs were rather conical, yellow, and placed singly on the leaf. The young larvæ when first hatched were greenish yellow and had rows of small dark spines, which disappeared after the first change of skin, and were replaced by the eight long filamentous appendages, which they kept until maturity.—H.F.]

PAPILIO SARPEDON, Linnæus.—(Plate XVII., ♀).

Papilio sarpedon, Linnæus, Syst. Nat., I., (10th ed.), p. 461 (1758); Mus. Ulr., p. 196 (1764); Syst. Nat., I. (12th ed.), p. 747 (1767); Cramer, Pap. Exot., II., pl. cxxii., figs. D, E (1779); Esper. Ausl. Schmett., pl. viii., fig. 2 (1785); Godart, Enc. Méth., IX., p. 40 (1819).

Papilio choredon, Felder, Verh. zool-bot. Ges. Wien, XIV., pp. 306, 350 (1864); Gray, Cat. Lep. Ins. Brit. Mus., I., p. 28, pl. iv., fig. 1 (1852).

Many years have passed since the day when, on one of our entomological hunts over the rich brush lands of Ash Island, we were so fortunate as to find a fine female of *Papilio sarpedon* laying her eggs upon the tender leaves and shoots of *Grijera salicifolia*. The discovery was the more welcome inasmuch as, although the butterfly itself was very familiar to us, the larva had hitherto eluded our search. Since then the cultivation of the Camphor tree (*Camphora officinalis*)—a tree which has proved excessively congenial as a food plant to *Papilio sarpedon*, *Papilio macleayanus*, and *Charaxes sempronius*—has become common, and any amateur entomologist may now easily capture the larvæ. The butterflies may be seen, during most of the fine summer days, darting to and fro about the Camphor trees, in the public parks and gardens near Sydney, in some instances so engrossed in the occupation of depositing their eggs that they may be captured with the hand. The eggs that we found at Ash Island were taken on the 14th March, and were hatched on the 19th of the same month; and evidently formed a part of the early brood of the succeeding summer, as the larvæ produced therefrom changed into chrysalids towards the end of April, and the butterflies did not take wing until the following November. The eggs are globular in form, pale yellow in colour, and are deposited singly on the leaves or shoots of the plant. The infant larva is rich black in colour, robust at the shoulders, and armed with numerous spines, similar to those of the larvæ of the Vanessæ; the pair on the shoulders are much larger than the others and are armed with branching setæ; there are also two pure white spines at the tail; head large, and yellow. As the larva increases in size it loses the whole of the spines with the exception of a black and white pair, short and pointed, on the sides of each of the three thoracic segments (those on the second segment being very minute), and the pair on the tail. The colour of the insect is now dull sap-green above, merging into a bluish ashy hue on the sides; a broad bright yellow band passes over the back of the third segment and connects the two shoulder spines. This general colouring is retained to full maturity, but the green becomes more subdued, and is finely speckled with white raised points, while the tail is pale lavender, and an undulating band of yellowish-white, fringed with fine hair, passes from it, over the feet, to the third segment; abdomen, thoracic feet and prolegs, ashy-white; head and caudal feet greenish; in length it measures 1¾ inches, is cylindrical, and thickest at the shoulders, gradually tapering to the tail; is sluggish in habit, but if irritated will rapidly protrude the retractile tentacula.*

The pupa, which was produced at the end of April, is attached by the tail and a median band, with the head upright—it measures 1¼ inch, is throughout light emerald green, finely speckled with darker, and with a row of dots above the spiracles; the upper part of head projects into a keel shaped process of considerable length, from which emanate four raised yellowish-white lines, proceeding down each side of the body and uniting at the tail; a similar raised line passes in front of the horn to the centre of head, which the imago, in emerging, splits exactly in half.

The butterfly measures from 3½ to 4 inches, and may be met with all through the summer.

The *Antennæ* ....(figs. 1 and 2) terminate in a hooked rather obtuse club, compressed near the apex, and slightly grooved.

The *Labial palpi* (fig. 3) small, scarcely projecting beyond the eye; above scaly, and beneath with longish hairs; basal and second joints equal, terminal small and globular.

The *Legs* : ....slender, very thinly covered with scales or hair, but with rows of small setæ on all the joints; tibiæ of intermediate and posterior pairs (fig. 4) with two small spurs at their apices.

Wings erect in repose.

The whole upper surface is silky jet black, with a broad transverse cerulean-blue band across the middle of both wings, tapering at each end; at the tip of upper wing this band breaks into small patches, and becomes faintly tinged with green. An outer row of cerulean-blue crescentic spots runs parallel to the margin of lower wing, which is produced and semi-caudate near the anal angle, and margined with black and white. Head, thorax, and abdomen, black, densely covered with fine greyish hair;

---

*[This description was taken from larva living, from the egg to maturity, under artificial conditions; and I am inclined to think that this must have caused considerable modifications of colour, as most of the full grown specimens I have subsequently found living on the Camphor Trees under natural conditions, exposed to full sunlight, etc., have been very bright grass-green above, paling into bluish-grey on the sides and tail, with head and foot pale yellowish green.—H.F.]

antennæ black. Beneath, dark bronze-brown replaces the black of upper surface, and the cerulean-blue of the band pales into a silvery pearly tint, divided by yellow nervules; the crescentic spots near the margin of lower wing are also silvery, and tinged with yellow at the anal angle; above these and near the discoidal cell are several wavy light crimson bars, and another short crimson bar with green above, near the base of the wing;* abdomen banded longitudinally with dark brown and yellowish-grey ; legs and front of head pale greenish-grey.

Illustrations are given of side and back of caterpillar, chrysalis, and upper and under surface of butterfly ; and its indigenous food plant *Geijera salicifolia*.

PAPILIO LYCAON, Westwood.—(Plate XVII., ♀).

Papilio lycaon, Westwood, Arcana Ent., II., p. 15 (1843) ; Felder, Reise Novara, Lep., I., p. 68 (1865).

Papilio eurypylus, Scott, MS.

Life-history : Mathew, Trans. Ent. Soc. Lond., 1888, p. 177.

We have invariably found the caterpillars of this *Papilio* feeding on the Custard Apple (*Anona cheremolia*), both in the suburbs of Sydney, and at the Hunter River ; and from the trees of this fine tropical fruit growing in the Sydney Botanic Gardens, and at Elizabeth Bay—the residence of the late Mr. W. Sharpe Macleay—we have for many successive seasons procured broods of the larvæ, and have carefully watched their development from the earliest stage, when the body is dark blackish-brown above, white beneath, and armed with many small spines, up through the various changes of skin to the final one, when the colour throughout is usually dark olive-green above, whitish beneath ; the head shining pale yellow, and six small black and white spines placed in pairs on the first, third, and caudal segment. During the intermediate changes of skin the larvæ vary considerably in colour, some being rich black or dark chocolate-brown, some bright brick-red, others again green ; they have also an additional pair of small spines on the second segment, which afterwards disappear. When quite mature the larva measures about 1¼ inch, is cylindrical and thickest at the shoulders, thence attenuating to the extremities ; sluggish in habit, and possesses the retractile tentacula.

The larvæ we collected near the end of January, changed to chrysalids early in March, and produced butterflies towards the end of the same month ; but those procured in March did not take wing until the following summer.

The chrysalis is attached by the tail and a median band, with the head upwards ; in length 1 inch ; pale emerald green throughout, finely spotted with darker green ; the thorax angular in front, with four slightly raised divergent lines proceeding down the sides of abdomen and uniting at the tail.

The butterfly measures about 3⅞ inches, but we have seen many specimens much smaller.

The *Antennæ* ....(figs. 1 and 2) terminate gradually in a club, compressed and slightly grooved near the apex.

The *Labial palpi* (fig. 3) small, projecting very little beyond the eye ; thinly covered above with scales, and beneath with longish hairs ; basal and second joints nearly equal in length ; terminal small, globular.

The *Legs* : ....slender, very sparingly clothed with scales, but with rows of small setæ on all the joints (fig. 4, anterior leg) ; intermediate and posterior pairs with two small spurs at apices of tibiæ.

Wings erect in repose.

The upper surface is silky jet-black. A broad transverse band of very pale greenish-blue passes through the centre of both wings, and is disconnected by the nervules and broken up into patches towards the tip of upper wing, where also several short transverse bars of the same delicate bluish-green occupy the discoidal cell ; a row of similarly coloured spots encircles the outer

*[In some specimens these bars are deep orange-yellow.—H.F.]

margins of both wings. The lower wing is fringed with black and white, and is not so much produced near the anal angle as in *P. sarpedon*. Head, antennæ, and thorax, black, with numerous fine greyish-blue hairs; abdomen brownish-black in centre, creamy-yellow at sides.

On the underside the markings are disposed exactly as above, but are larger and more confluent, and have a pearly, silvery hue. Rich bronze-brown replaces the black of the upper surface, and the lower wings are enlivened by four short, bright crimson bars, relieved by dark brown at the discoidal cell, from whence they proceed to the anal angle and there unite with a crimson band bordering the inner or abdominal margin; there is also a short crimson bar near the base of the wing. Legs and front of head very pale bluish-grey; abdomen banded longitudinally with brown and creamy-yellow.

Three stages of the larvæ are figured on some young foliage of the *Anona*, also the chrysalis, and upper and under surfaces of perfect insect.

OPHIUSA (?) FRONTINUS, Donovan.—(Plate XVIII.)

Papilio frontinus, Nat. Hist. Ins. New Holl., pl. 32, fig. 2 (1805).

Agarista frontinus, Boisduval, Voy. Coquille, Zool. II., p. 282 (1826); Voy. de l'Astrolabe, Lep., pt. I., p. 173 (1832).

Noctua scapularis, Guérin, Voy. Coquille, Atlas, Ins. pl. 19, fig. 2 (1826).

Spanoceola atroia, Scott, MS.

These caterpillars were very abundant at Ash Island in the beginning of March, feeding on the *Breynia oblongifolia*, several stages of growth being occasionally found on the same shrub. They are full loopers, and possess only twelve feet, the pairs usually found on the sixth and seventh annulations being absent; they rest with the body placed close against the branch or stem, and if touched drop quickly to the ground and there remain in hiding: the same colouration prevails from youth to maturity, but becomes more subdued with increasing age, the full grown larva having the whole upper portion to a little above the spiracles, light, bright, lavender, covered with longitudinal rows of fine black dots, and, on the side of each segment—with the exception of the first—a large oval orange-yellow patch, with intermediate distinct black spots; the lower or abdominal half is creamy-white minutely speckled with black; while a row of black dots divides the lavender and cream coloured portions; spiracles black; head and feet creamy-white, with numerous black dots and patches on the former; body long, cylindrical, attenuating very slightly towards the extremities, and measuring about 2¼ inches.

Towards the close of March the caterpillars prepared their cocoons by weaving together several leaves of the *Breynia*, and forming inside them an oval cocoon, close in texture and of greyish-white colour, in which they remained during the winter, taking wing in the ensuing September.

The chrysalis (fig. 1) is about 1 inch long, moderately stout in form, of a dark plum colour, and thickly covered with whitish bloom.

The perfect insect measures about 2 inches.

The *Antennæ* ....setaceous; covered above with small scales; in male (fig. 2) with clusters of cilia beneath, continued to the apex which is terminated by a few setæ (fig. 3); in female pubescent beneath, and the apex terminating in a double seta.

The *Labial palpi* project forwards and upwards to a level with the top of eye (fig. 4); second joint nearly twice as long as basal or terminal which are about equal in female, but in male the terminal is slightly longer and more acute (fig. 5); basal and second joints thickly covered with feathery scales, the terminal only moderately so.

The *Legs*: ....anterior pair (fig. 6) much smaller than the others; intermediate pair with two, and posterior pair (fig. 7) with four strong spurs on tibiæ; tibiæ and femora thickly clothed with hair; tarsi with close scales above and a few setæ beneath.

Wings deltoid in repose; moth nocturnal, but if disturbed during the day flying with great rapidity to a fresh place of concealment.

The whole surface above is silky jet black—about the middle of the upper wing is a broad transverse pure white band, slightly dentate on the outer margin and having a small black ear-shaped mark at the end of the discoidal cell; there are also a few faint whitish subcostal streaks, and, towards the anal angle of lower wing, an indistinct whitish spot; margins of both wings scalloped with white; head and neck bright tawny-orange; thorax black with tawny hairs; abdomen black, in male tufted with orange at the tail. Underside bronzy-brown, with white margins. Legs with the femora densely tufted with orange coloured hairs.

The caterpillar on *Breynia oblongifolia*, and the moth, are figured in the illustration.

OPHIUSA MYOPS, Guenée.—(Plate XVIII.)

Ophiusa myops, Guenée, Spec. Gen. Lep., Noct., III., p. 263 (1852); Walker, Cat. Lep. Het. Brit. Mus., Noct., XIV., p. 1426 (1858).

Catocala fusca, Scott, MS.

This is a rare species, as during many years spent in collecting Lepidoptera at Ash Island, we only found a couple of the larvæ, which were feeding in company with the preceding species, *Ophiusa (?) frontinus*, in March, on the *Breynia oblongifolia*. Like the *O. frontinus*, the caterpillar rests with the body extended at full length, close to the branch; but it differs greatly from that species in appearance and conformation, being subdued in colouring and having all the feet present, although the pairs on the sixth segment are considerably smaller than the others; there are also two small pointed yellowish protuberances on the eleventh segment. When full grown it measures 2 inches, is elongated, rather flat beneath, and attenuates very slightly towards the head; the colour throughout light pinkish-brown finely sprinkled with black, becoming rather darker on the back; on the side of the fourth segment is a yellowish spot, shaded with dark brown outside, and with a brown centre; the spiracles and a few spots over the legs are also brown; head, thoracic and caudal feet, pale yellow with brown markings; prolegs pinkish-brown, spotted with black.

About the middle of April the caterpillars connected together some leaves of their food plant, by coarse silken threads, and formed inside of these a strong silken cocoon, sufficiently large to hold the chrysalis, which measured 1 inch (fig. 1). The chrysalis is dark plum colour, thickly coated with whitish bloom, rather stout in form, and blunt at the head.

In August the moths took wing; they measured about 2¼ inches in expanse, both being females.

The *Antennæ* ....setaceous, covered above with scales, below slightly pubescent, and with a lateral row of minute setæ (fig. 2).

The *Labial palpi* second joint half as long again as either basal or terminal, which are nearly equal; basal and second joints thickly covered with feathery scales, terminal only moderately covered, and rather obtuse at apex; the whole project forwards and upwards not quite even with the top of the eyes (fig. 3).

The *Legs:* ....anterior pair rather small; intermediate pair with two (fig. 4), and posterior pair with four, strong spurs on tibiæ; tibiæ of all thickly clothed with feathery scales; tarsi with small scales, and rows of small setæ beneath.

Wings decumbent in repose; moth nocturnal.

The entire upper surface of the moth is dusky brown, shaded and speckled with darker, having on the middle of upper wing a broad transverse chocolate-brown bar bordered by a narrow ochreous-yellow line: this bar is deeply sinuated on the outer margin, and here connects with a somewhat triangular patch of dark brown, also edged with ochreous-yellow, which proceeds from the apex of the wing; near the base are two wavy transverse ochreous lines. The nervules across the disc of lower wing are ochreous, and close to the margin near anal angle is a dusky triangular patch shaded outwardly with dark brown; margins dusky: head, thorax, and abdomen dusky brown, the thorax crested with dark brown hairs. Underside uniform dusky brown.

The *Breynia oblongifolia* is again figured, with larva and female moth.

FODINA OSTORIUS, Donovan.—(Plate XVIII.)

Phalæna ostorius, Donovan, Nat. Hist. Ins. New Holl., pl. xxxii., fig. 3 (1805).
Agarista ostorius, Boisduval, Voy. de l'Astrolabe, Ent., p. 173 (1832); Walker, Cat. Lep. Ins. Brit. Mus., I., p. 41 (1854)
Fodina ostorius, Walker, Cat. Lep. Het. Brit. Mus. Noct., XIV., p. 1430 (1858).
Anocala sabbatistica, Scott, MS.

The caterpillars of this pretty moth exhibit great diversity in colour and markings, and we have figured two as examples of types frequently met with. They were found by us in tolerable abundance at Ash Island in the months of January and March, sometimes feeding on the Nerium or Oleander trees, but more frequently on the indigenous *Marsdenia suaveolens*. For the purpose of illustrating the differences in colour and markings alluded to, we will describe three varieties: In No. 1 the colour is light yellowish-green, with the head, and a distinct lateral band close to the spiracles, light gamboge-yellow; on each side near the back is a row of small black spots ringed with white, two on each segment; and there are rows of smaller black spots, one on each segment, both above and below the yellow lateral band. The spiracles and tips of thoracic feet, rusty red. No. 2 is throughout pale bluish-emerald green, with head, lateral band, and two dorsal patches on the eleventh segment, bright gamboge-yellow. Along the back, arranged in pairs on each segment are short black annular bands edged with white, curving slightly inwards at their ends. Between these and the lateral band there is a row of distinct black spots, two on each segment, with the exception of the thoracic segments which have only one spot on each; a similar row of spots over the feet. No. 3 is dull pale bluish-green, with yellowish head, and wants the lateral band and dorsal yellow spots. The black annular bands are much enlarged, and almost unite with the black spots above the spiracles. The lower row of black spots are also enlarged into patches of irregular form which continue over the feet, and under the abdomen. When full grown the caterpillar measures a little over 1½ inches, is cylindrical and plump, and attenuates very slightly at the extremities. Those found early in March changed to chrysalids at the end of the month, weaving a slight cocoon encrusted with earth on the surface of the ground, and in this they passed the winter, taking wing the ensuing November. The chrysalis (fig. 1) is shining reddish-black, ⅞ inch in length, rounded at the head, and slightly widest in middle.

The moth measures 2 inches in expanse.

The *Antennæ* ....setaceous; covered above with feathery scales, below pubescent; the female with a double row of setæ commencing at some distance from the base, and continued to the apex; in the male (fig. 2) the setæ commence near the base and are longer than those of the other sex.

The *Labial palpi* large and long (fig. 3); second joint three times, and terminal more than twice, as long as basal (fig. 4); terminal slender, and pointed at apex; the whole moderately clothed with feathery scales, and a few long hairs near the base; project forwards and outwards, not quite level with the top of eye.

The *Legs*: ....intermediate pair with two, and posterior pair (fig. 5) with four, strong spurs on tibiæ; tibiæ of all thickly covered with long scales, tarsi moderately so, and with a few rows of fine setæ beneath.

Wings deltoid in repose; moth nocturnal, but if disturbed can fly swiftly in daytime.

The ground colour of superior wing is very dark blackish-brown, strikingly relieved by various quaint cream coloured markings, disposed as follows—one, bifid in form, proceeds from the base of the wing, passes in a nearly straight line below the costa, and unites at right angles with a broad diagonal band which takes its rise near the hinder angle, and strikes the costa a little beyond the end of discoidal cell; a second band broken in the middle by blackish-brown runs along the outer margin, and passing round the hinder angle, proceeds in a narrow line to the base of the wing. The wing is slightly falcate at the tip, and lengthened at the posterior margin. The inferior wing is also blackish-brown, but not so dark as the superior; on the disc is an oval cream coloured spot, and on the margin near anal angle, a cream coloured semi-circular marking somewhat resembling a horse shoe with black centre; the wing is rather small, and slightly irregular in outline. Head, thorax, and abdomen, blackish-brown, the thorax with two transverse creamy bands; the abdomen with annular rings of orange-yellow. The imago produced from No. 3 caterpillar showed some trifling varietal differences about the lower wings; the oval spot on disc, and the patch near anal angle being bright ochreous-yellow, and the latter having a distinct black spot in centre; the abdomen is also almost entirely yellow above, black beneath, and tufted with black at the extremity. The underside dark brown; fore wing with a broad central transverse cream coloured fascia, a spot at the apical and at the hinder angle. Hind wing with markings as above, but larger and more distinct.

Two caterpillars are shown on some foliage of the *Marsdenia suaveolens*, and the perfect insect is also figured.

OPHIUSA SENEX, Walker.—(Plate XVIII).

Ophiusa senex, Walker, Cat. Lep. Het. Brit. Mus., Noct., XV., p. 1832 (1858).
Catocala albo-fasciata, Scott, MS.

This is by no means a common insect, and very few specimens have hitherto come into our possession, and these only from Ash Island, where we found the larvæ, in February, feeding on the native Ash tree (*Elæocarpus obovatus*). It usually lies extended close to the bark, to which it assimilates so exactly in colour as to render detection very difficult. Although the feet are all present, the pair on the sixth segment are slightly inferior in size to the others, and this, combined with the elongation of the fourth, fifth, and sixth segments, causes the caterpillar to loop slightly when in the act of walking. When fully extended it measures 2¼ inches, is attenuated in form and rather flat beneath, of a light fawn colour covered with longitudinal rows of minute black dots and striations, those above the stigmata forming two wavy bands; on the eleventh segment is a small double protuberance, tipped with yellow and outlined with black, and on each side near the back is a row of small black spots, one on each segment; head fawn colour mottled with brown dots and striations, arranged in bands; thoracic feet yellowish.

The cocoons were formed in March, and consisted of a coarse silken web, covered externally with fragments of earth and dried leaves. The chrysalis (fig. 1) is about 1 inch long, moderately stout, rounded at the head, and throughout dark shining reddish-black.

The moth did not take wing until the following December; it measures a little over 2 inches in expanse.

The *Antennæ* ....setaceous, stem covered with scales above, beneath pubescent, with a lateral row of small setæ; the tip (fig. 2) terminating in a horny seta emitting a few hairs.

The *Labial palpi* basal and terminal joints equal in length, second joint nearly twice as long; basal and second joints thickly covered with feathery scales, terminal only moderately scaly; rounded at the apex: the whole projecting forwards and upwards until even with the top of the head (fig. 3).

The *Legs*: ....anterior pair comparatively small; intermediate pair with two, and posterior pair with four rather large spurs; tibiæ of the anterior and posterior pairs thickly covered with feathery scales, second pair only moderately so, but in the male this joint is provided at the base with a large fan-like tuft of long hairs (fig. 4), which can be concealed in a groove at the side of the joint; tarsi all moderately hairy and with a few rows of setæ.

Wings decumbent in repose; insect nocturnal.

The superior wing, with the exception of a portion of the outer margin which is inclosed within a convex line which passes from the tip to about one-third of posterior margin, is rich chocolate-brown, relieved by a broad white transverse bar, widest at the costal and posterior margins, and there finely speckled with purplish-brown; a second short transverse bar of dark olive-brown edged with white intersects the chocolate-brown close to the tip, which is slightly falcate; the remainder of wing between the outer margin and chocolate-brown is olive-brown, with an indistinct scalloped line, and a row of small brown spots following the outline of margin. The inferior wing is dark neutral-tint, with a wavy whitish band across the disc, and a large whitish patch clouded with black, near the anal angle; marginal border whitish; head and thorax dark brown; abdomen olive-brown banded with darker; antennæ white above, brown beneath. Underside fawn coloured, suffused with darker externally, and with numerous dark wavy transverse lines.

The caterpillar and moth are represented, with the *Elæocarpus obovatus* in seed.

EXPLANATION OF PLATE XVI.

PAPILIO ANACTUS, Macleay.

Larva and Pupa.—Fig. 1, Antenna. Fig. 2, Head, palpus, and proboscis, side-view. Fig. 3, Labial palpus. Fig. 4, Hindleg.

Food-plant: *Citrus aurantium.*

EUPLŒA CORINNA, Macleay.
(DANAIS CORINNA, on plate.)

Larva and Pupa.—Fig. 1, Antenna. Fig. 2, Head, palpus, and portion of antenna, side-view. Fig. 3, Labial palpus. Fig. 4, Foreleg. Fig. 5, Hindleg.

Food-plant: *Maralepis suaveolens.*

EXPLANATION OF PLATE XVII.

PAPILIO SARPEDON, Linnæus (Female).

Larva and Pupa.—Figs. 1 and 2, Antenna from above and below.
Fig. 3, Head, palpus, and portion of antenna, side-view. Fig. 4, Hindleg.

Food-plant: *Geijera salicifolia*.

PAPILIO LYCAON, Westwood.

(PAPILIO EURYPYLUS, on plate.)

Larva and Pupa.—Figs. 1 and 2, Antenna from above and below.
Fig. 3, Head, palpus, and portion of antenna, side-view. Fig. 4, Foreleg.

Food-plant: *Anona cherimolia*.

EXPLANATION OF PLATE XVIII.

OPHIUSA (?) FRONTINUS, Donovan.
(SPARGOALA ATRATA, on plate.)

Larva.—Fig. 1, Pupa. Figs. 2 and 3, Portions of antenna of male. Fig. 4, Head, palpus, and portion of antenna, side-view. Fig. 5, Labial palpus, male. Fig. 6, Foreleg. Fig. 7, Hindleg.

Food-plant: *Breynia oblongifolia*.

OPHIUSA MYOPS, Guenée.
(CATOCALA FUSCA, on plate.)

Larva.—Fig. 1, Pupa. Fig. 2, Portion of antenna. Fig. 3, Head, palpus, and portion of antenna, side-view. Fig. 4, Hindleg.

Food-plant: *Breynia oblongifolia*.

FODINA OSTORIUS, Donovan.
(ANOGALA CAUDALISTICA, on plate.)

Larva and Variety.—Fig. 1, Pupa. Fig. 2, Portion of antenna, male. Fig. 3, Head, palpus, and portion of antenna, side-view. Fig. 4, Labial palpus. Fig. 5, Hindleg.

Food-plant: *Marsdenia suaveolens*.

OPHIUSA SENEX, Walker.
(CATOCALA ALBO-FASCIATA, on plate.)

Larva.—Fig. 1, Pupa. Fig. 2, Portion of antenna. Fig. 3, Head, palpus, and portion of antenna, side-view. Fig. 4, Intermediate leg, male.

Food-plant: *Elæocarpus obovatus*.

OCNERIA HELIASPIS, Meyrick.—(Plate XIX., ♂ and Underside).

Ocneria heliaspis, Meyrick, Trans. Roy. Soc. South Australia, XIV., p. 192 (1891).
Chelepteryx expolitus, Scott, MS.

We have found this species upon different occasions at Manly Beach, close to the entrance to Port Jackson; and also at other spots situated within a radius of ten miles from Newcastle, on the Hunter River. In every instance the caterpillars were solitary, living in exposed positions upon the low bushes of young *Eucalypti*. Our Hunter River specimens were found in January, February, and April; and those from Manly Beach in February.

The female caterpillar measures nearly 3 inches, the male 2½ inches, and there is very little difference in colouring between the sexes. The body is cylindrical, and of almost uniform thickness; the ground colour pale pinkish-drab, with a fringe of short, stiff, yellowish hair between each segment, and another down the back. Each segment bears a whorl of six cushion-shaped tubercles which emit clusters of stiff hair, about a quarter of an inch long, and either yellowish, rusty-red, or creamy-white in colour; and there are two additional reddish hairs, nearly one inch long, proceeding from the centre of each cluster. Placed near the dorsal line are two small tubercles—one on each side of each segment—also emitting clusters of hair, with the exception of the pair on the fourth segment which bear upright pencils of stiff rusty-red hairs about half an inch long. There are a few additional tubercles on the neck, and on the caudal segment, causing the anterior and posterior extremities to be nearly hidden by the long stiff fringes of hair. The head is dark rusty-red, with a few pinkish-drab markings; the thoracic feet dark rusty-red, the abdominal and anal claspers pinkish-drab, with markings of dark rusty-red. One of our specimens, a full-grown female larva, was more ochreous in colour, and the short stiff fringe of hair down the back was creamy-white, and gave the appearance of a dorsal band.

Some of the larvæ formed their cocoons early in February, the others about the middle of March, or later on. Some fresh leaves of the Eucalyptus were drawn together and fastened securely with coarse yellowish silk, which for additional security was woven some distance up the foot stalks and stem of the twig; inside the leaves an elongated oval cocoon was then formed, of a dirty white colour and strong texture, lined inside with silk. Some of our moths took wing in March and April, but a few specimens remained in the cocoons for a period of ten months.

The chrysalis (fig. 1, male) measures about 1 inch; the female about 1¼ inches. It is throughout a light pinkish-drab, with the wing cases, antennæ, and segments outlined with purplish-brown.

In expanse the female moth measures 3½ inches; the male 2½ inches.

Ocneria heliaspis, Meyr., ♀

The *Antennæ* ....(fig. 2), male, rather strongly bipectinate, the pectinations ciliate, and each terminating in a seta. Female very slightly bipectinate, the pectinations exceedingly small near the base of the antennæ.

The *Labial palpi* (fig. 3), male, small; projecting forwards and slightly downwards. In male, the basal and second joints are nearly equal in length, the terminal small, and rather obtuse at the apex (fig. 4, denuded of hair). The whole covered above with longish hairs and scales. In female, the basal and terminal joints are nearly equal; the second joint is almost twice as long as either basal or terminal; the whole very sparingly covered with hairs and scales.

The *Maxillæ* ....obsolete.

The *Legs*: ....anterior pair (fig. 5, male) spurless; intermediate and posterior pairs (fig. 6, male) each with two small spurs at the apex of tibiæ. The tibiæ and tarsi moderately hairy, the hairs thickest on the tibiæ of anterior pair. A few rows of small setæ on the tarsi, and some longish hairs beneath the femora.

The wings are semi-deltoid in repose, the anterior angle of the lower wing projecting slightly beyond the costal margin of the upper wing. Moth nocturnal.

In colouring the sexes are very dissimilar, the female presenting a very sober, quaker-like appearance beside her richly-hued mate. The upper wing of female is elongated, and the costal and exterior margins slightly arched; the apical angle rather pointed. The whole upper surface is light olive-grey, suffused with dull purplish-brown near to the anterior angle of lower wing; two rather indistinct transverse bands of brownish-black, forming shallow scallops within the interspaces of the veins, cross the wings a little beyond the front of the discoidal cell, which bears, near its apex, a distinct brownish-black spot; there is also a small blackish spot on each vein, where the lower row of scallops intersect. The margins are entire and fringed with grey cilia. The abdomen is stout, and projects as far as the anal angle of the lower wing. Beneath, the colouring is light silvery olive-grey, suffused with purplish-brown on the disc of the upper wing. The discoidal spot is larger than on the upper surface, and the inner transverse band is distinct, but the outer line of scallops is very faint.

The male* has the costal margin of the upper wing nearly straight, the apical angle rather pointed, and the exterior margin somewhat indented. The upper surface is a rich warm orange-brown; the upper wing with many transverse zig-zag fasciæ of dark brownish-black colour, and a black discoidal spot. On the under wing the zig-zag fasciæ are very dark near the anal angle, but faint across the disc. The abdomen is rather short, and black at the extremity. Antennæ blackish-brown. On the under side the upper wing is orange-brown near the base, very dark brown along the exterior margin, and dull olive-brown near the apical angle; the transverse fasciæ are very indistinct, but the blackish discoidal spot is present. The lower wing is reddish-orange near the abdominal margin, and olive-brown at the exterior portion. There are two indistinct transverse fasciæ below the disc, and a dark discoidal spot. Thorax and abdomen reddish-orange; head and legs olive-brown. The male is very active in its movements, and if alarmed dashes itself about with such violence that its plumage is quickly destroyed.

Our illustration shows the caterpillar and its cocoon on a sprig of *Eucalyptus*, with the upper and under surfaces of the male moth.

DARALA HAMATA, WALKER.—(Plate XIX., ♀).

Darala hamata, Walker, Cat. Lep. Het. Brit. Mus., pt. IV., p. 895 (1855).
Eulophocampa anaxia, Scott, MS.

This exceedingly showy caterpillar is by no means common at the Hunter River, where our specimens—in all about half a dozen—were obtained. Some of these were found in March, at Tomago, a settlement about ten miles from the Port of Newcastle; and others were taken in June near East Maitland, twenty miles from Newcastle. In every instance the caterpillars, like those of the *Oenetria heliaspis*, were solitary, feeding in exposed positions upon the young shoots springing from the stumps of the Eucalyptus trees which had been felled during the process of clearing the land for cultivation.

The full-grown caterpillar attains to 3½ inches, and is cylindrical, elongated, and densely pilose above; beneath smooth, and velvety-black, with a central longitudinal band between the legs, composed of bars and spots of straw colour. From the third to the eleventh segment the body is covered above with dense short hair, like velvet pile, bright chestnut-red in the centre of the segments, but almost black at the sides, near the segmental divisions. On the posterior edge of each segment are five plumes, or brushes, of fine hair nearly half an inch long and of extreme whiteness and purity, the centre or dorsal row being wedge-shaped, and, like the others, bending gracefully backwards towards the tail of the caterpillar. On each segment, immediately in front of these white plumes, is an annular row of round yellow tubercles, four in number, each emitting a bunch of stiff shortish hair, either chestnut-red or black in colour, and also a few white hairs nearly an inch in length. Below the stigmata, and in a line with the four yellow tubercles, are smaller round tubercles arranged in pairs, and below these again, close to the feet, is another small tubercle. All these tubercles emit bunches of shortish chestnut-red, black, or white hairs. There is also a tubercle near the centre of the segments, on each side of the dorsal line, and from these tubercles on the fourth segment proceed long pencils of white hair. The three anterior and two posterior segments are also tuberculated, but are so densely pilose that the tuberculations are not visible. Anteriorly the thick fringes of black or white hairs—some half, and others fully one inch long—bend forwards in an inverse direction to the silky-white plumes, and form a sort of double ruff which completely hides the head. The posterior

---

* [Mr. Meyrick's description of the male (Trans. Roy. Soc. S. Australia, XIV., p. 192) was drawn up from Mr. Scott's original specimens, now in the collection of the Australian Museum].

extremity is similarly concealed by long thick hair, and consequently unless the caterpillar is in movement, the proper identification of head or tail is nearly impossible. The head is dark blackish-brown; thoracic feet dark reddish-brown; abdominal and anal claspers reddish-brown with straw coloured markings. The male larva is similar, but rather darker in colour, and measures about three inches.

Two of the caterpillars found in March, prepared for the chrysalis state early in April, exhibiting great restlessness and a desire to escape from confinement; moving about incessantly for two days until they became almost exhausted. One finally spun its cocoon beneath a piece of dried bark, attaching to it sundry small twigs—the other selected the corner of the feeding cage. A loose web of yellowish silk was first spun in various directions, as an outer support, and then inside this several other layers of silk were woven, having the hairs of the caterpillar sticking through; each of these layers was of distinct formation, and could be peeled off separately. Within these outer envelopes was the cocoon itself, rather oval in form, lightish brown in colour, and strongly coriaceous in texture; the interior beautifully smooth and satiny, and with a small slit at the upper end, apparently for the more easy exit of the moth.

The chrysalis (fig. 1, female) measures 1¼ inches in length, and a little under half an inch in width; the male is about 1 inch, and more slender. It is throughout light bistre-brown, darker near the abdominal divisions, the wing-cases, head, etc.

The moths took wing in the middle of the February of the following year. The female measures slightly over 3¼ inches; the male 2½ inches.

The *Antennæ* ....(fig. 2) male, moderately bipectinate throughout; pectinations finely ciliate, and each terminating in a seta. Of the female, rather short, thin, and with very small bipectinations (fig. 3).

The *Labial palpi* in male (fig. 4) project upwards, nearly even with the top of the eyes; in female very small, bending slightly downwards. In male the basal and second joints are twice the length of the terminal, which is rather obtuse at apex; in female the basal joint is slightly longer than the second, and rather acute at apex (fig. 5, denuded of hair). The whole moderately hairy in the male, but less so in the female.

The *Maxillæ* ....obsolete.

The *Legs*: ....anterior pair spurless (fig. 6, female); intermediate and posterior pairs (fig. 7, male) with two short spurs at apices of tibiæ. The whole moderately hairy, but with the hairs thickest on the tibiæ of anterior pair; a few rows of small setæ on the tarsi, and some long hairs beneath the femora of the male.

The wings are semi-deltoid in repose, the anterior angle of the lower wing projecting slightly beyond the costal margin of the upper wing. Moth nocturnal.

The upper wing of the female moth is elongated, the costal margin arched, with the apical angle produced and rather falcate, and the exterior margin much rounded. The lower wing is slightly produced at both the apical and anal angles, and has the exterior margin rounded. The general colour of the upper surface is drab, tinged with pale brown along the exterior margins, and with dark brown at the base of both wings. Two wavy bands or fasciæ of ochreous-yellow bordered with dark brown pass transversely across both wings, commencing near the middle of the interior margins, and terminating with a slight curve, on the costal margin in front of the discoidal cell. The outer of these bands is scalloped near the interior margin of the upper wing, and relieved behind with rich brown, but the scallops become very indistinct towards the apical angle. On the lower wing the scallops are very regular and are continued across the wing, the rich brown background bringing them into strong relief. A wavy brown border incloses the dull olive-brown basal portion of the wings, and inside this, on the upper wing, is a second wavy dark band. There are also two brownish patches near the apical angle of upper wing, and a distinct dark discoidal spot. The antennæ are yellowish above; the head very small, and like the thorax and abdomen, drab-coloured; the latter being stout and projecting a little beyond the lower wings. Margins of all the wings fringed with short yellowish cilia. On the under side the female is uniformly silvery-drab, and the transverse fasciæ are very faint in colour. The legs all bear a conspicuous silvery-white spot near the junction of femora and tibiæ.

In the male the upper wing is rather triangular, and not arched on the costa, or rounded at the exterior angle, as in the female. The general colour and markings are very similar to those described in the female, but are lighter. There are also two dark discoidal spots, one placed behind the other. The thorax and abdomen are very pilose; the latter is rather short, not extending beyond the lower wings, and tufted with brown hairs at the extremity. The under side is silvery-drab, with two faint fasciæ, and two distinct brown discoidal spots on each wing. The antennæ, front of head, thorax and abdomen, are yellowish; legs brownish, with silvery-white spot on each femur. In both sexes the basal half of the wings is very pilose on both the upper and under surfaces.

The illustration shows the female caterpillar and moth.

PAPILIO STHENELUS, W. S. Macleay.—(Plate XX., ♀).

Papilio sthenelus, W. S. Macleay, King's Survey, Austr., II., p. 457 (1827); Boisduval, Spéc. Gén., Lep., I., p. 239 (1836); Semper, Mus. Godf., XIV., p. 42 (1878).

Life-history: *Papilio erithonius (auct.)*, Mathew, Trans. Ent. Soc. Lond., 1888, p. 169.

Towards the end of October, we found at Ash Island, on the tender shoots of an orange tree, some eggs and a few very young larvæ of the *Papilio sthenelus*. The eggs were globular, and pale greenish-yellow, and were placed singly on the leaves. The little larvæ were at first very dark blackish-brown in colour, and armed with annular whorls of spines branching like those of the *Pyrameis* and *Junonia*. At the second change of skin these spines become smaller, and at the third change they disappear, and are replaced by two rows of small dark spines, one on each segment, placed near the back; there are also very small additional spines on the sides of the three anterior segments. At this stage the ground colour of the larva is shining dark brown, with a dorsal band of dull orange spots, and on each side of the body, near the head and tail, and also over the abdominal feet, are irregular clusters of spots of the same dull orange hue; the feet are dark brown, the head black, with a yellowish divisional marking. As the larva increases in size the ground colour gradually turns into dull green, with longitudinal spots or patches of yellow, and finally it becomes a rich velvety sap-green, very dark along the back, but paler and of a slightly bluish tint at the sides. The dorsal rows of spines have now disappeared, and in their place are small raised points; a pair of largish yellow tubercles project from the first segment over the head, and a similar pair from the caudal extremity. In the centre of segments four to eleven is an annular band of six conspicuous spots of saturnine-yellow, the lowest row strongly outlined with black; on the third segment the lowest spot of this annular band is absent, while the upper ones are almost confluent, and have in front, exactly in the centre of the segment, a pair of small black spots, ringed with white. On the second segment the saturnine-yellow spots are very faint, and they do not appear at all on the first segment. A second annular band, composed of alternate black and faint white patches, is placed on the front of each segment close to the divisions, and on the second and third segment this band forms an almost continuous black pattern over the back; beneath it, over the thoracic feet, are several black spots of irregular form. A whitish lateral band passes over the legs to the caudal extremity, which is also whitish, and has on it several small black spots. The abdominal feet are whitish, thickly speckled with brown; the thoracic feet and head shining yellowish-green.

In length the full-grown caterpillar measures a little over 1¾ inches, is cylindrical and robust in form, especially at the shoulders, is sluggish in habit, but if irritated rapidly protrudes the retractile tentacula.

A few of our specimens varied in some respects from those described above, the ground colour being yellowish, and the black spots between the segmental divisions and over the feet being more strongly defined.

At the end of November the caterpillars changed into chrysalids, previously attaching themselves to some convenient support by the tail and a silken median band. The chrysalis is slightly over 1¼ inches in length, is throughout of a light pinkish-brown colour, covered with minute dots of brown and black. The head is bifurcate and projecting; the thorax armed on the back with an angular projection; and the abdomen ridged dorsally and laterally.

The butterflies took wing in December, January, and February. The female measures 3¾, the male about 3½ inches.

The *Antennæ* ....terminate in an elongated club, pointed at the apex, and very slightly compressed laterally (fig. 1).

The *Labial palpi* very small (fig. 2), project slightly in front of the head; basal and second joints about equal in length (fig. 3); terminal joint very small and globular; the whole covered with fine scales, and rather long hair in front.

The *Legs*: ....Anterior pair (fig. 4) with a horny sac on the inner side of tibiæ; intermediate and posterior pairs (fig. 5) with two small spurs on tibiæ; tibiæ and tarsi of all the legs nearly naked, but with several longitudinal rows of small black setæ.

Wings erect in repose.

The ground colour of the upper surface of this butterfly is silky black, with many large patches of dark cream colour arranged transversely across the centre of both wings, and a row of kidney-shaped spots running parallel to the exterior borders. Across the discoidal cell, and also between it and the apex of the superior wing, are various cream-coloured patches of irregular form and size, the one placed between the fourth and fifth subcostal nervules having in its centre a circular black spot with faint bluish pupil*; the base of the wing is thickly covered with clusters of minute cream-coloured scales arranged in parallel lines. A

---

*[In some specimens this silvery-bluish pupil is absent.—H.F.]

very conspicuous spot of light orange-red, with silvery-blue above, occupies the anal angle of the inferior wing, and a similar but rather smaller and darker spot is placed on the anterior angle, under the costal vein. Near the apex of the discoidal cell, and on the disc below it, are delicate patches of silvery-blue scales, and the base of the wing is thickly covered with short silky cream-coloured hairs. The thorax and abdomen are dark in the centre, and cream-coloured on the sides, and there are several round creamy spots on the head and behind the eyes.

The cream-coloured markings on the under side of the superior wings are disposed exactly as on the upper side, but are larger and more confluent, and the black background is duller and slightly bronzed. Near the anterior margin five of the spots or patches, extending from the third sub-costal to the first median vein, are dull ochreous-yellow, and the costa is also tinged with yellow. The under surface of the inferior wing is almost entirely rich cream-colour, suffused with pale yellow at the basal half. The spots and patches are similar to the upper surface in their arrangement, but the black background only shows as an outline to these, and on the denticulated margin. Placed across the disc, and beneath the discoidal cell, extending from the first subcostal to the third median nervule are dull orange-yellow patches, with bars of black and silvery-blue above; the large ocellular spot near the anterior angle is also encircled with black and silvery-blue; thorax, abdomen, and legs, cream-coloured, the former covered with dark hairs.

This attractive *Papilio* is not very common in the neighbourhood of Sydney, but we have collected it in considerable numbers at the Hunter River, where its favourite feeding-grounds were the fields of blue lucerne and clover. It is, however, a species of wide distribution, being found in Queensland, South Australia, and Victoria, as well as in New Guinea.*

The caterpillar and chrysalis are represented on the Orange (*Citrus aurantium*), with both the upper and under surfaces of the female butterfly.

PAPILIO MACLEAYANUS, Leach.—(Plate XX., ♀).

Papilio macleayanus, Leach, Zool. Misc., I., pl. v. (1814); Godart, Enc. Meth., IX., p. 47 (1819); Hubner, Zutr. Ex. Schmett, f. 501, 562 (1825); Semper, Mus. Godf., XIV., p. 45 (1878).
Papilio scottianus, Felder, Verh. Zool.-bot. Ges. Wien, XII., p. 489 (1862); Reise Novara, Lep., I., p. 73 (1868).

Our first observations upon the life-history of this beautiful insect, the *Papilio macleayanus*, were carried out at Ash Island, when we observed the female butterfly depositing her eggs on the leaves of *Grijera salicifolia*. The egg is somewhat globular in shape, light pearly-green in colour, and placed singly on the leaves and young shoots of the food-plant. When the young larva first emerges from the egg, its body is nearly black on the sides, with a broad whitish dorsal line, interrupted by two transverse black bands, one anteriorly, passing over the shoulders between the second and third segment, and one posteriorly, between the eleventh and twelfth segment. On the first and twelfth segment are pairs of large black tubercles with a tuft of hairs at the extremity, similar to those on the larva of *Anthenea*; and, on each of the remaining segments, is a whorl of six small black bifid bristles; on the second and third segment, the bristle in the second row on each side is replaced by a large black tubercle like those near the head and tail, making in all eight tubercles on the body, four on each side. The head is black; the feet and under side of body whitish, with a fringe of fine black hair along the side. A marked difference accompanies the first change of skin: the body is then a very delicate green, slightly speckled with darker green; the head and first segment pale yellowish. The whole of the bifid bristles have disappeared, and in their place are rows of small white spots, while on the three anterior segments are short horny reddish-black projections in place of the large tubercles; a broad band of dark chocolate-brown passes over the shoulders between the second and third segments, and there is a narrow band of the same colour near the tail, which terminates in a white bifurcate projection. At this stage the body is distinctly pyriform in outline, being robust anteriorly, and much attenuated posteriorly. When resting the caterpillar erects the anterior segments. At the third and fourth change of skin the colouring is more pronounced, being a bright yellowish-olive, rendering the white spots more conspicuous. The anterior segments are yellow, tinged with reddish, and the shoulder bands and spines are deep reddish-brown. The pair of spines on the third segment are still conspicuous, but those on the first and second segments are very small; the bifurcations at the tail are yellow, tipped with black. The retractile tentacula are readily protrudible at this stage. During the succeeding changes of skin the

---

* [Mr. G. F. Mathew, in describing this species under the name of *Papilio erithonius*, Cram., states that it was very common in the Botanic Gardens, Brisbane, in September, 1882; and at Port Moresby, New Guinea, in November and December, 1884, he found quantities of the larva feeding upon a species of *Salvia*. His larva and chrysalids, however, do not exactly agree with ours in colouring, but we are inclined to think that the differences are merely varietal.]

colour becomes a more decided green; the rows of white spots are fainter, and the dark shoulder band is scarcely seen; the spines —with the exception of the pair on the third segment—have disappeared. Finally, the larva, which now measures nearly 1¼ inches, and is very plump and onisciform, is, on the upper side, intensely vivid grass-green, minutely punctured with darker green; and on the under-side delicate bluish-green. The pair of shoulder spines are dark brown, short, and sharp, and from the base of each a narrow yellowish-white line passes along the side of the body to the bifurcate tail; beneath this line is a row of small white spots —one on each segment—and a delicate fringe of white hair over the feet; the head is small, and shining grass-green. The bifurcations at the tail now lie parallel, and appear like a single projection, and the anterior segments are usually drawn together and bent down instead of being held erect as in the earlier stages.

At the end of March our caterpillars underwent the change into chrysalids, attaching themselves in the usual way to some suitable support, by the tail and a silken medium band. The chrysalis measures 1 inch, is delicate emerald-green in colour, very finely speckled with darker green, and with two small oval reddish spots placed near the middle of the back, and a smaller reddish spot behind the eyes. The thorax bears a conspicuous keel-shaped projection, from which several yellowish ridged lines diverge, one passing straight in front of the head, the others on each side of the wing-cases and abdomen, and uniting at the tail.

The butterflies took wing in May. Most of the specimens averaged 3 inches in expanse, but we have caught an occasional specimen about ¼ inch larger.

The *Antennæ* ....terminate in a short and slightly hooked club (fig. 1).

The *Labial palpi* small, projecting forwards slightly in front of the head (fig. 2); second joint twice the length of basal (fig. 3, divested of hair); terminal joint very small and rather globose; the whole covered above with fine scales and thickly fringed below with hair.

The *Legs*: ....anterior pair (fig. 4) with a horny sac on the inner side of tibiæ; intermediate and posterior pairs each with two small spurs at the apex of the tibiæ (fig. 5); tibiæ and tarsi nearly smooth, and with several longitudinal rows of small black setæ.

Wings erect in repose.

On the upper surface both wings are broadly margined with rich silky black; on the inner or basal half they are light greenish-white, which deepens into a rich light apple-green on the discoidal cell and costa of upper wing. Adjoining the costa of the upper wing, placed transversely, are two large light green patches, one wedge-shaped, near the end of discoidal cell, the other of oblong form, nearer to the apex of wing; and two small spots between the nervules, just below the discoidal cell. A row of greenish-white spots, one between each nervule, runs parallel to the exterior margins of both wings—occasionally these spots are very faint on the lower wing, appearing only in a few scattered scales. The lower wing is prolonged near the anal angle into a graceful and slightly spatulate tail, and is fringed at the anal angle and on the abdominal margin with salmon-coloured hairs. The margin of the upper wing is entire, but the lower wing has alternate denticulations of black and white. Abdomen greenish-white; thorax and head, brownish-green, the head being very hairy in front. On the under surface the markings are disposed as above, but the rich black of the border is replaced by bronzy-brown, delicately varied with a pearly sheen near the apex of the upper wing and near the undulating margin of the lower wing. The green colour is very vivid near the costa of the upper wing, and over the whole basal half of the lower wing, which has the anterior margin bordered with red at the base and near the apical angle. Three of the marginal rows of spots near the posterior angle of the upper wing are united at the veins, and the two small greenish-white spots below the discoidal cell are also united and form a single V-shaped marking. The abdomen is greenish-white; the legs light apple-green; the antennæ tipped with orange. The sexes are alike in colouring.

Like the larva of *Papilio sarpedon*, the larva of the *Papilio macleayanus* has of late shown a decided preference for the leaves of the camphor laurel, and in the neighbourhood of Sydney is usually found feeding upon that tree, although we have heard of its having been found on the orange tree. The butterfly is bold and rapid in its movements, and forms a beautiful and graceful object when sipping the sweets of the flower garden, or darting swiftly in mid-air. Its distribution is wide, extending to Lord Howe Island, Norfolk Island, Tasmania, Victoria, and in Queensland as far north as the Johnstone River.

Three stages of the larva, on the leaves of the *Geijera salicifolia*, the chrysalis, and upper and under views of the perfect insect are given in the plate.

SELIDOSEMA THERMÆA, Meyrick. (Plate XXI, ♂)

Selidosema thermæa, Meyrick, Proc. Linn. Soc., N.S. Wales, 1891, p. 600 (1892)
Geometra cameli-pila, Scott MS.

Several larvæ of this species were found at Ash Island in January, feeding on the *Cupania anacardioides*, and we subsequently obtained a few others in Sydney on the foliage of the *Acacia decurrens*. In length the larva is about 1¼ inches, cylindrical and moderately slender; the feet are ten in number, the ninth segment only being provided with abdominal claspers; on the eleventh segment there are two short but distinct dorsal projections, and the head is slightly bifid and pointed. The general colour of the body is dark olive-brown, with numerous fine brown annular rings. A band of pale ochreous-yellow, spotted with white, passes along each side over the legs, but becomes very indistinct as it approaches the head and tail; this band is edged with brown on both sides, and beneath it on each segment is a velvety-black oblong patch. The dorsal portion above the band is longitudinally striated with dark reddish-brown, and there are a few whitish streaks, running parallel to the band, from the fifth to the ninth segments. The fifth segment is slightly enlarged, and has on each side a black spot placed diagonally near the centre of the band. Head olive-brown, striated with dark reddish-brown, and with a faint yellowish streak on each side; thoracic and anal feet brown, marked with reddish; abdominal claspers brown, with an ochreous patch spotted with white adjacent to the lateral band.

The cocoons were formed of coarse silk covered with fine particles of earth, and were placed a little below the surface of the ground. The chrysalis (fig. 1, male) measures about half an inch, is rather slender in outline, and throughout a shining reddish-brown. Some of the moths took wing in August, and others in the beginning of February.

The perfect insect expands 1¼ inches.

The *Antennæ*:........ male (fig. 2) deeply bipectinate throughout, the pectinations finely ciliated; female filiform.

The *Labial palpi* moderately large (fig. 3 male, and 4 denuded of hair): middle joint nearly twice as long as basal, and four times as long as terminal joint; terminal very slender, and acute at the apex. The whole covered with hair and scales, and projecting forwards and upwards about level with the top of the eyes.

The *Legs*: ....male and female, long and slender; intermediate pair with two, and posterior pair (fig. 5, male) with four, thin spurs on the tibiæ. The whole thinly covered with scales.

The wings are horizontal in repose.

The whole upper surface of the male is chestnut-brown, covered with many short transverse reddish-brown striæ: these striæ are more numerous near the margins and across the costa, making these portions appear darker than the disc of the wings. A few blackish-brown transverse fasciæ of very irregular outline occupy the centre of both wings, and there is a small blackish-brown spot on the disc of the upper wing. Margins slightly undulating, and outlined with blackish-brown. Head, thorax, and abdomen, chestnut-brown, striated longitudinally with reddish-brown; antennæ reddish-brown, with yellowish pectinations. The underside is silvery-brown, clouded with bronze-brown near the hind margins. A distinct brown spot on the disc of both wings, and a silvery-white patch at the apical angle of the upper wing. In the female moth the space between the transverse blackish-brown fasciæ on the upper wing is of a steely neutral-tint, shaded with rich brown on the inner portion, and near the disc, and there are some additional dark brown patches near the apical angle. The basal half of the lower wing is steely neutral-tint, striated with dark brown; and there is an irregular band, formed of short transverse striæ, near the anal angle.

The illustration represents the leaf and ripe seed capsules of the *Cupania anacardioides*, with the caterpillar and male moth.

SELIDOSEMA GILVA, Scott, MS.—(Plate XXI, ♂).

Geometra gilva, Scott, MS.
Boarmia psychastis, Meyrick, MS.

The caterpillars of this pretty species feed indiscriminately on the leaves of the *Acronychia Baueri* and the *Olea paniculata*. Some of our specimens, which were captured at Ash Island in February, exhibited great diversity in colour, some being light apple-green, and others pale pinkish-drab. The green larvæ were larger in size, and probably would have produced female moths, but unfortunately a species of *Ichneumon* destroyed them before they underwent their second change. The male caterpillar is about 1 inch and 3 lines in length, is cylindrical, rather elongate, with two small projections near the tail, and with only one pair of abdominal claspers which are placed on the ninth segment. The ground colour is light pinkish-drab, covered with fine continuous longitudinal lines of dark brown; a row of small brown spots on each side, above the stigmata; stigmata whitish, with yellow centres; head with pale drab streak on each side, and striated in front with dark brown. The green variety had a conspicuous black spot on each side of the fifth segment, a dorsal row of faint white spots, and two small white spots on each side of the bifurcate tail. About the middle of February the caterpillars prepared their cocoons of silk, covered with agglutinated earth, just below the surface of the soil, and early in March the perfect insects took wing.

The chrysalis (fig. 1, male) is 7 lines in length, and throughout light shining reddish-brown.

The male moth measures a little over 1¼ inches.

The *Antennæ* :........male, rather strongly bipectinated to about three-fourths of its length, each pectination finely ciliate and terminating in a rather incurved seta (fig. 2).

The *Labial palpi*: male (fig. 3 and fig. 4, denuded of hair), moderately large; basal joint twice as long as middle joint, terminal joint small, slender, and rather obtuse at apex. Basal portion very thickly covered with scales and hair, terminal very thinly covered. The whole projecting forwards, about level with the top of the eyes.

The *Legs* ....rather long and slender. Intermediate pair with two, and posterior pair (fig. 5, male) with four longish spurs on the tibiæ; tibiæ and tarsi closely covered with feathery scales, and with a long fan-shaped bunch of hair near the base of tibia of posterior leg.

The wings are horizontal in repose.

The upper surface of the male moth is creamy-white, delicately speckled with pinkish-brown. Five thin wavy blackish-brown fasciæ pass transversely across the upper wing, and between the first and second, and fourth and fifth, of these fasciæ, is a faint band of pale ochreous-yellow. The lower wing has three similar fasciæ, the pale ochreous-yellow band being between the third and fourth. A row of small blackish spots runs parallel to the exterior margin, which is slightly undulating, and bordered with creamy-white cilia. Antennæ, head, thorax, and abdomen, creamy-white, with blackish-brown bars on the patagia, and a double row of blackish-brown spots down the back of abdomen; base of thorax, and tail, pale ochreous-yellow. The under side is creamy-white with a silvery lustre. Near the apical angle of both wings is a bronze-brown patch, darkest on the upper wing; and there is also a brownish discoidal spot.

The flowers and fruit of the *Acronychia Baueri* are figured, with two larvæ and the male moth.

SELIDOSEMA LUXARIA, Guenée.—(Plate XXI., ♂).

Hemerophila luxaria, Guenée, Spec. Gén. des Lépid., Vol. IX., p. 220 (1857).
Tephrosia disperdita, Walker, Cat. Lep. Het. Brit. Mus., XXI., p. 416 (1860).
Selidosema luxaria, Meyrick, Proc. Linn. Soc. N.S. Wales, 1891, p. 699 (1892).
Geometra recte-fasciata, Scott, MS.

This is rather a common species in the neighbourhood of Sydney, where it may be found in October and November feeding upon the pretty *Leptospermum scoparium*. The female caterpillar measures a little over 1¼ inches; the male slightly under. The body is cylindrical, and very little attenuated; the prevailing colour a light pinkish-drab, shaded with grey, and with many thin, longitudinal black striæ and spots, darkest on the sides of the seventh and eighth segments and near the head. About the middle of each segment, near the back, are two very small spines or projections, the pair on the fifth segment being rather the largest; the eleventh segment is slightly tuberculated. The head is pinkish-drab, striated and spotted with black; the apex is rather acute. The abdominal feet are absent, with the exception of the pair on the ninth segment.

In November the cocoons were formed, and like the species previously described, were of silk covered externally with fine earth, and placed near the surface of the ground. The chrysalis (fig. 1) measures ½ inch, and is shining yellowish-red.

The moths emerged in December and January. The female measures 1 inch and 8 lines, the male 1 inch and 5 lines.

AND THEIR TRANSFORMATIONS.   35

The *Antennæ* ....long; bipectinated to the tip in both sexes. In the female (fig. 2), the pectinations are very small; in the male (fig. 3), rather long; in both finely ciliated.

The *Labial palpi* small, particularly in the female (fig. 4, male). Basal joint long, being twice the length of the middle joint; terminal joint very small, and rather pointed (fig. 5 denuded of hair). Basal and middle joints moderately covered with hair and scales. In the male, projecting forwards in front of the eyes; in the female, bending down.

The *Legs* ....slender; anterior pair small (fig. 6, female); intermediate pair with two, and posterior pair (fig. 7, male) with four, thin and rather long spurs on the tibiæ. Tibiæ and tarsi moderately covered with scales and fine hair; the male with a fan-shaped tuft of long hair beneath the base of the tibia of the posterior leg.

The wings horizontal in repose.

The upper surface of both sexes is whitish-grey, sprinkled with minute dots and lines of brown and black. A double fascia, black above and very dark brown beneath, proceeds from the inner margin of both wings, about one-third from the base, and running almost parallel to the costa, terminates on the hind-margin, just below the apical angle; a similar but fainter fascia is placed near the hind-margin, and the space between these fasciæ is darkly shaded with brown and black. Two thin, transverse fasciæ, one brown, the other black, are near the base of the wings, which also bear a small brown discoidal spot; the outer margins are denticulated, and are outlined with black; marginal fringe grey and brown. Thorax and abdomen grey, shaded with black and brown; a black band crosses the thorax, and is continued for some distance below the costa of upper wing. The male has a few annular bands of dark brown on the back of abdomen.

The under side is light silvery-brown, shaded with dark bronze-brown near the hind margins. There are a few faint, transverse brownish fasciæ, and a brownish discoidal spot on each wing.

The caterpillar is shown on its food plant, the *Leptospermum scoparium*, together with the female moth.

SELIDOSEMA DESTINATARIA, Guenée.—(Plate XXI, ♂).

Gnophos destinataria, Guenée, Spec. Gén. des Lépid., Vol. IX., p. 297. (1857).
Boarmia attenis, Walker, Cat. Lep. Het. Brit. Mus., XXI., p. 390 (1860).
Tephrosia indirecta, Walker, Cat. Lep. Het. Brit. Mus., XXI., 418 (1860).
Tephrosia vagaria, Walker, Cat. Lep. Het. Brit. Mus., XXVI., p. 1542. (1862).
Selidosema destinataria, Meyrick, Proc. Linn. Soc. N.S. Wales, 1891, p. 613 (1892).
Geometra lentiginosa, Scott, MS.

Of the few specimens of this caterpillar which have come into our possession, some were found in May in the Botanic Gardens, Sydney, on the leaves of the common *Convolvulus;* others were discovered at Ash Island in October, on a vine of the *Stephania hernandiæfolia.* The caterpillar is in length 1¼ inches, is cylindrical and moderately slender; the abdominal feet absent, with the exception of one pair on the ninth segment. The body is reddish clay-colour, with many short longitudinal striæ and spots of purplish-brown; near the stigmata is a faint lateral band, containing a small white spot on the fifth and sixth segments; beneath this band, on each segment, is a short streak of purplish-brown, and there is also a purplish-brown oblique marking on the terminal segment. The head is clay-colour, with a faint marking on each side, and striated in front with purplish-red.

The cocoons were formed of coarse silk, covered externally with particles of earth, and were placed close to the surface of the soil. The chrysalis (fig. 1, male) is barely half an inch in length, and shining reddish-brown in colour. The moths took wing in July and December.

The female measures 1 inch and 4 lines; the male slightly less.

The *Antennæ:*........male, rather long; bipectinated to the apex, each pectination finely ciliated (fig. 2); female, filiform.

The *Labial palpi* small, especially in female (fig. 3, male). Basal joint large, and twice as long as middle joint; terminal joint very small, thin, and acute at the apex (fig. 4, male); basal and middle joints rather thickly covered with feathery scales and hair. The whole projecting forwards and slightly upwards.

The *Legs* ....slender; intermediate pair (fig. 5) with two, and posterior pair with four, rather long, thin spurs on the tibiæ. Tibiæ and tarsi thinly covered with feathery scales.

Wings horizontal in repose.

The upper surface of both sexes is of a silvery-cream colour, with many fine pinkish and yellowish-brown scales, and some minute blackish dots and short transverse black striæ, scattered over the surface. Three irregular black fasciæ pass transversely across the wings; on the upper wing the middle fascia, beyond the basal two-thirds, is strongly upturned; the outer fascia is denticulated, the denticulations being shaded with black; a black patch of irregular form is placed between the second and third fasciæ, considerably beyond the discoidal cell. The outer margins are strongly denticulated, and outlined with black. The head, thorax, and abdomen are cream-colour, with occasional scales of pink and yellowish-brown colour, and the abdominal divisions are clearly outlined with black. The under side is silvery cream-colour, brownish on the costa, and near the apical angle; three brownish fasciæ pass transversely across both wings, which are outlined with brown, and have a brown discoidal spot.

The caterpillar and male moth are figured, with the *Stephania hernandiæfolia* bearing clusters of parti-coloured seeds.

EXPLANATION OF PLATE XIX.

OCNERIA HELIASPIS, Meyrick (Male).
(Chelepteryx repolitus, on plate).

Larva.—Fig. 1, Pupa. Fig. 2, Portion of antenna of male. Fig. 3, Head, palpus, and portion of antenna, side-view. Fig. 4, Labial palpus, denuded of hair. Fig. 5, Foreleg. Fig. 6, Hindleg.

Food-plant: *Eucalyptus, sp.*

---o---

DARALA HAMATA, Walker.
(Eulophocampa amœna, on plate.)

Larva.—Fig. 1, Pupa. Fig. 2, Portion of antenna of male. Fig. 3, Portion of antenna of female. Fig. 4, Head, palpus, and portion of antenna, side-view (male). Fig. 5, Labial palpus, denuded of hair. Fig. 6, Foreleg (female). Fig. 7, Hindleg (male).

Food-plant: *Eucalyptus, sp.*

EXPLANATION OF PLATE XX.

PAPILIO STHENELUS, W. S. Macleay.

Larva and Pupa.—Fig. 1, Antenna. Fig. 2, Head, palpus, and portion of antenna, side-view. Fig. 3, Labial palpus. Fig. 4, Foreleg. Fig. 5, Hindleg.

Food-plant: *Citrus aurantium.*

PAPILIO MACLEAYANUS, Leach.

Larvæ and Pupa.—Fig. 1, Antenna. Fig. 2, Head, palpus, and portion of antenna, side-view. Fig. 3, Labial palpus. Fig. 4, Foreleg. Fig. 5, Tibia of hindleg.

Food-plant: *Geijera salicifolia.*

EXPLANATION OF PLATE XXI.

SELIDOSEMA THERMÆA, Meyrick.
(GEOMETRA CAMELI-PILO, on plate).

Larva.—Fig. 1, Pupa. Fig. 2, Portion of antenna of male. Fig. 3, Head, palpus, and portion of antenna, side-view. Fig. 4, Labial palpus, denuded of hair. Fig. 5, Hindleg (male).

Food-plant: *Cupania anacardioides.*

SELIDOSEMA GILVA, Scott, MS.
(GEOMETRA GILVA, on plate).

Larva.—Fig. 1, Pupa. Fig. 2, Portion of antenna (male). Fig. 3, Head, palpus, and portion of antenna, side-view. Fig. 4, Labial palpus, denuded of hair. Fig. 5, Hindleg (male).

Food-plant: *Acronychia Baueri.*

SELIDOSEMA DESTINATARIA, Guenée.
(GEOMETRA LENTIGINOSA, on plate).

Larva.—Fig 1, Pupa. Fig. 2, Portion of antenna (male). Fig. 3, Head, palpus, and portion of antenna, side-view. Fig. 4, Labial palpus, denuded of hair. Fig. 5, Intermediate leg.

Food-plant: *Stephania hernandiæfolia.*

SELIDOSEMA LUXARIA, Guenée.
(GEOMETRA RECTE-FASCIATA, on plate).

Larva.—Fig. 1, Pupa. Fig. 2, Portion of antenna (female). Fig. 3, Portion of antenna (male). Fig. 4, Head, palpus, and portion of antenna, side-view. Fig. 5, Labial palpus, denuded of hair. Fig. 6, Foreleg. Fig. 7, Hindleg.

Food-plant: *Leptospermum scoparium.*

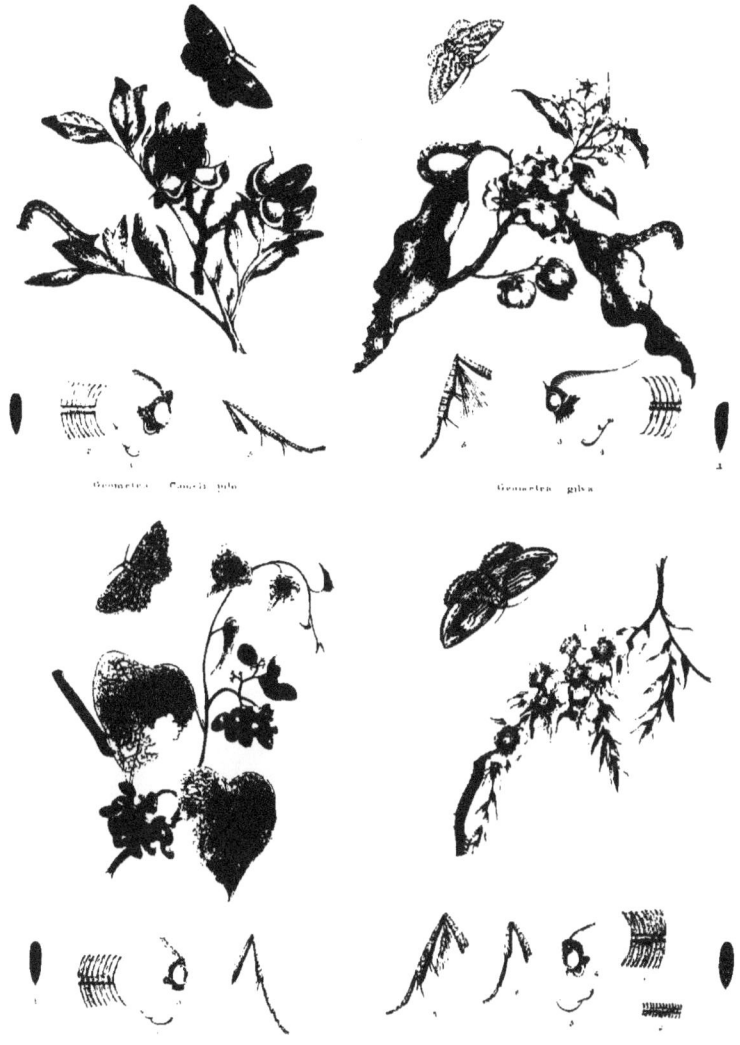

www.ingramcontent.com/pod-product-compliance
Lightning Source LLC
Chambersburg PA
CBHW020243090426
42735CB00010B/1818